Praise for *Tutoring Matters*:

"America is in the midst of a wave of volunteerism. Academic tutorial programs are at the leading edge of this commitment by average Americans to improve failing institutions. This book offers a scholarly and practical perspective on tutoring both as an art and [as a] science. It is a must read for those who hope to be effective tutors, for those who intend to establish serious tutorial programs, for educators and policy makers."
—**Walter R. Allen,** Professor of Sociology and African American Studies, UCLA

"This is a much needed book for everyone who is called upon to assist others in the process of learning and discovery. There is much wisdom and guidance and I for one found much of value for my own work, even after 30 years of teaching. . . . It is an empowering guide for each and every one of us who is engaged in the task of teaching and learning."
—**Helen S. Astin,** Professor, Graduate School of Education, Associate Director of HERI, UCLA

"I direct a Community Service Learning Program at the University of Michigan which includes a tutorial program. This book is the most practical, concrete, appealing and intellectually coherent preparation material I have seen. We will use it, not only in our school tutorial program, but also in our work with juvenile detention systems and the homeless. Its focus on the tutor, as well as on the tutee, makes it an excellent stimulus for reflexive learning."
—**Mark A. Chesler,** Professor of Sociology and Director of Community Service Learning Programs, University of Michigan–Ann Arbor

"We train approximately 75 tutors each year in western Kansas. By accident we stumbled on [*Tutoring Matters*]. It has become an invaluable resource that addresses the theory, technique, and emotion of tutoring. *Tutoring Matters* is a winner!"

—**Joni Clark,** Director, Americorps Kansas Heartland Literacy Program (HeLP)

"*Tutoring Matters* is a wonderful addition to the many books on tutoring. . . . Most books and manuals on tutoring and mentoring are 'how to' guides on teaching techniques and activities. They suggest that the tutor is entering into a hierarchical relationship to give something to someone who is somehow deficient. *Tutoring Matters* captures what I have learned from more than 20 years of working with college aged tutors—tutors often learn more than they teach if properly prepared. *Tutoring Matters* not only discusses how to tutor. It also helps a tutor learn how to learn. The book is wonderfully grounded. [It] uses the situations and the words of the many tutors whose field notes formed the basis of the book. For the novice tutor, these scenarios are almost as good as being there and will make the first visit far less intimidating. For the experienced tutor, the scenarios will be reassuring confirmation that they are not alone in their fears, frustrations, insecurities, and insights. Don't get me wrong, the book is packed with wonderful ideas as to how to tutor more effectively but, in my opinion, occupies a unique place among 'how to' books by focusing as much on the internal state of the tutor as the process of assisting another person. I believe that tutoring is distinguished from teaching by the nature of the personal relationship that is built between the tutor and his or her charge. This book makes that point with crystal clarity."

—**Richard Cone,** Executive Director, Joint Educational Project, University of Southern California

"Essential strategies; key insights. A 'must have' sourcebook for literacy tutors."
—**Robert W. Maloy**, co-author of *The Essential Career Guide to Becoming a Middle and High School Teacher* and *Schools for an Information Age*

"[*Tutoring Matters*] is as much about tutoring—teaching and learning—as it is about relationships. This book does a marvelous job of preparing potential tutors for the joys and challenges of tutoring, and of connecting meaningful[ly] with people who may be vastly different from them. But the authors do more than prepare tutors to teach; through poignant vignettes and judicious advice, they prepare tutors to form relationships and, in the process, to learn more about themselves."
—**Sonia M. Nieto,** Professor of Education, University of Massachusetts–Amherst

"What the novice tutor needs is reassurance. That is exactly what *Tutoring Matters* offers through the accounts of others who have attained it and by the concrete details that are so clearly presented in this book."
—**Wilbur Rippy,** Professor of Education, Graduate Programs, Bank Street College of Education in New York City

"This book targets and solves the many [problems] between tutors and clients with insight and sensitivity."
—**Selma R. Zimmerman,** Mentor Teacher, New York City Board of Education

Tutoring Matters

Temple University Press
Philadelphia

Tutoring Matters

Everything You

Always Wanted to Know

about How to Tutor

Jerome Rabow, Tiffani Chin,
Nima Fahimian

Temple University Press
Copyright © 1999 by Temple University
All rights reserved
Published 1999
Printed in the United States of America

Text design by Kate Nichols

Library of Congress Cataloging-in-Publication Data

Rabow, Jerome.
    Tutoring matters : everything you always wanted to know
about how to tutor / Jerome Rabow, Tiffani Chin, Nima Fahimian.
        p.   cm.
    Includes bibliographical references.
    ISBN 1-56639-695-6 (alk. paper). — ISBN 1-56639-696-4
(pbk. : alk. paper)
    1. Tutors and tutoring—United States—Handbooks,
manuals, etc.   I. Chin, Tiffani.   II. Fahimian, Nima.   III. Title.
LC41.R33 1999
371.39′4—dc21   98-33360

Contents

Preface and Acknowledgments

We would each like to begin by describing how we came to write this manual and by thanking the people who made it possible.

Jerry Rabow

This manual probably began some thirty years ago when I was shocked to discover what was going on with my children in one of the "better" public schools in Los Angeles. As a new professor in my first teaching position at UCLA and the father of two young boys, I deliberately settled close enough to a public school with a reputation for excellence.

I took it for granted that "excellence" was just that, a series of good teachers, academically high standards, and the most advanced technology for learning. But what I discovered in this "excellent" public school was something else entirely, which is illuminated by three pivotal incidents.

The first incident occurred when my youngest child told us that he was required to lie down on his mat so that he and all the other children could "benefit" from rest period. At that point I began to wonder about the professed standard of excellence. How could teachers or administrators assume that all children wanted and needed rest at the same time? Was this really for the children's benefit? This was the beginning of my understanding of the horrors of public education in the United States. Schools tend to standardize all. The rules are unmistakable: you fit in, and you conform.

I found the second event, a few years later, even more disturbing. My older son was participating in the required run around the track and was sent home for wearing boxer shorts. He was told that since his boxer shorts were hanging one inch below his gym shorts, he was being sexually provocative. He was also told that we, his parents, must purchase jockey shorts. I could not accept this. I went to the school with my son and argued with a gym teacher who wore short sleeves and no tie—an outfit he would have been sent home for when I was growing up. We were told by the principal and the gym teacher that the boxer shorts were too provocative to young women in this "excellent" junior high school. Neither the principal nor the teacher was able to respond favorably to my comments about shifts in norms and etiquette or about individual taste and freedom of choice. My son took his demerit. The banality and stupidity of rules based on such standards was impressed upon me. But even more disturbing was the attitude that came across loud and clear: there will be no questioning the rules. The rules are for your own good. We know what is best for you. The idea that children might know what is good for them is unthinkable.

The third incident took place when my son stayed home because of a religious holiday. The teacher gave an important exam on this holiday and would not allow any make-ups to the ten children who stayed at home. The punishment for religious beliefs was the final blow to my faith in public education. I realized that something must be fundamentally wrong with public education in this country. Schools seemed to cultivate conformity and obedience, destroy passion and initiative, and have little respect for difference.

It was then that I began my process of self-education. I was determined to teach my students that there were better ways to

teach and learn. I elected to teach a sociology class in my department, and with the advantage of never having studied the sociology of education, I could start fresh with my own self-education,
and I did. In the sixties, a set of critics/writers were deeply critical
of public education, and I read them assiduously. Herb Kohl,
Jonathan Kozol, Neil Postman, John Holt, Paolo Freire, and Sylvia
Ashton-Warner documented the horrors of public education and
illuminated ways in which children should be taught. These
readings led me to some of the classic thinkers in the field, such as
John Dewey, A. S. Neill, Plato, and Aristotle. Reading and my
teaching led me to collaborate with a colleague and a graduate
student to write *Cracks in the Classroom Wall* (Robischon, Rabow,
and Schmidt, 1991). The book was historical and critical but did
not offer much in the way of tangible direction for students desirous
of enacting change.

By this time I was requesting that my students tutor as part of
their educational experience and bring their tutoring problems to
my classroom for discussion. Although satisfying and educational,
these minilessons and lectures proved to be limited in scope. Out
of my dissatisfaction, the idea for this book started to take hold.
Some ten years ago I began telling students to take notes when they
tutored. Before these notes could be transformed into a tutoring
manual, four more events had to transpire.

The first event involved a young student, Nima Fahimian, who
took an honors course with me entitled "Freud, Fairy Tales, and
Feminism," then a class in education, where he took up the tutoring process that I required of all my students. His confrontation
with a tutee who seemed unwilling to learn presented him with a
challenge, and the challenge provided him with a direction. His
interest in and dedication to public school children continued for
four years in conjunction with his UCLA education and courses in
his pre-med major. His effort to help me collect notes and work with
tutors by organizing their tutoring schedules and matching tutees'

hours and needs with tutors' hours and needs made the tutoring venture less chaotic and more focused.

Coinciding with Nima's efforts came strong support from the UCLA Office of Instructional Development, the second major event that led to the development of this tutoring manual. This office, under the leadership of Parvin Kassai, assigned Cynthia Chavez to work with me. Together they helped to bring about a coherent tutoring venture.

A third event had to do with the publishing of an excellent book, *Writing Ethnographic Field Notes* (1995), by Robert Emerson, Rachel Fretz, and Linda Shaw. This book encouraged students to develop an awareness beyond the content of their note taking. We brought the authors' ideas to class, looked at various tutoring incidents in light of their categories, and found the students thinking more critically about what they were doing.

A fourth event was the arrival of Tiffani Chin, the second author of this manual, in graduate school at UCLA in the sociology department in 1996. She was a grader for my undergraduate class in education. Her grasp of the tutoring issues, sensitivity to students and their note-taking process, and passion about education made the final contribution toward making this book a reality. We now had field notes galore, two very involved and concerned students, and myself. Out of this combination would come a tutoring manual.

Although I am concerned about many aspects of U.S. life, I am especially concerned about the way we teach and educate our children. I hope this manual will contribute to a better education for all, one that encourages and supports the development of deep interests, passions, freedom of choice, freedom of expression, and all other human potentialities.

By now a number of tutees have grown and have entered adulthood. Ingrid and Amanda Castro, tutees who came to America speaking not a word of English, have gone on to college. They call me every year to thank me for what their tutors gave them. May all tutors have such an experience.

This manual is dedicated to all children, but especially to Matthew and Zachary Rabow and Lucie Carolina Berman, the grandchildren that Roslyn Rabow and I share and who enrich my life—only a part of what I am so lucky to have with Roslyn.

Tiffani Chin

I've been tutoring for the past seven years. In two instances, it's been my job, working with upper-middle-class students on homework and test prep. The other two times I've tutored, I've been a volunteer working with inner-city elementary and high school students in Los Angeles. Although tutoring gets easier with every experience, I'm always left with unanswered questions. I can say with no hesitation that I've never entered a tutoring situation without wondering, "Aren't they going to show me what to do?"

My most recent foray into tutoring has involved working with a group of high-school-aged guys, recently on parole from L.A. County lock-up. I remember sitting in the warehouse that had become our tutoring center and asking the coordinator to come up with writing topics for me to give the students. I had been tutoring for years and was in the middle of writing this manual. Still, I was certain that I couldn't come up with writing prompts that would be compelling to minority teenage boys whose experiences on the streets, in gangs, and in jail had set their lives spinning in vastly different directions from my protected, middle-class, academic existence. What if they thought I was stupid? What if I offended them? What if I made them angry? What if I just flat out bored them?

But in the end, I not only came up with my own writing topics, I did it because I came to understand, and in some ways befriend, this group of guys I previously would have feared. They taught me simple knowledge, such as slang terms for drugs and crimes and how to read graffiti tags. But I also learned something about why a kid would become a Crip and what it's like for one gang member to pick a fight with a crosstown rival. I will never again listen in the same way to a newscaster or a politician or a policeman talk about gangs. Working with those kids taught me a lot about a group of people whom everyone talks about but who rarely get a chance to speak for themselves.

And that's one of the best parts of tutoring. You gain insights into people and situations you would never have been exposed to otherwise. Whether it's gang life or just the everyday life of a second-grade boy, it opens up a whole new world. It's also a way to get your hands dirty, to really do something. I like to be able to voice my opinion in social and political debates, and I feel that my tutoring gives me a greater right to do it. Tutoring has been my way of putting my effort where my mouth is.

I began graduate school, the path to spending my life in sociology, because I wanted to study social issues and problems. I tutor because I want to play a role in solving them. In writing this manual, I'm thrilled to be able to play a part in empowering others to do the same.

I would like to thank Jerry and Nima for allowing me into their project. I want to thank all of my tutees, past and present, for it is their work with me that lies behind all the insights I have lent to this book. Thanks also to Bob Emerson, who has taught me many of the skills and techniques that went into the creation of this manual. Most of all, I want to thank my family, especially my mom, who have supported me in everything I've ever wanted to do.

To all future tutors—I wish you luck, and the joy that tutoring has given me.

Nima Fahimian

The motivation behind writing this tutoring manual was cultivated by my own frustrations and struggles in educating children. What seemed a relatively simple task in 1993 soon became a challenge that only my patience and understanding of the significance of my role as a tutor could overcome. Having tutored university students throughout my college career, I felt confident about taking the opportunity to tutor children at Mar Vista Family Center in Culver City—a nonprofit, community-based organization involved in educating and counseling immigrant, poor, and minority families. I soon realized that my extensive university-level knowledge in a multitude of academic areas was not enough to tutor the two second graders assigned to me.

Shocked by this first experience, I employed every theory and view I had read in Peter McLaren, Mike Rose, Sylvia Ashton-Warner, Paulo Freire, and others discussed in Professor Jerome Rabow's education courses, in which students' field experiences were heavily emphasized. I was fortunate to have Professor Rabow's approach to education and his philosophy of experiential learning as my guiding principles. I then learned from experience and from my tutees how to put my knowledge and skills to work. Soon I realized that my education was a tool, subject to modifications and transformation through real-life experiences, and I suspect this is what Professor Rabow wanted me to learn.

By contributing to this tutoring manual, my hope is that some of you will develop strong feelings about education in this country. As George Dennison mentions in his book, *The Lives of Children*, we do not need genius to bring life into education. What we need are leaders with strong vision who respect children and their right to freedom of choice. We need leaders who can realize children's energy and are willing to promote their curiosity and willingness to explore what is genuinely exhilarating to them.

I thank Professor Rabow for his guidance and friendship. I also appreciate the great work and expertise of Tiffani Chin that helped produce this manual. The hard work and generosity of all the sociology students and tutors who contributed their notes throughout the years must be recognized, although there are too many to mention by name here. I thank my father and mother, Dr. Parviz and Mina Fahimian, for all their support and effort to understand me and let me grow. Most of all, I acknowledge the great work of Ms. Sarah Z. Ter-Minasyan in establishing the "Saturday Tutorial Program" and thank her for her most valuable friendship.

Tutoring for me has been a journey that presented many unexpected challenges and learning experiences, while allowing me to touch individuals whom I would never otherwise have met or found something in common with. Tutoring is a lot like medicine: I am amazed every day when I discover a connection between what I did as an undergraduate and what I do now as a medical student, and I'm sure the same connection will manifest itself when I become a physician.

I hope you enjoy this book and allow yourselves to learn from your tutees and colleagues.

The three of us would like to thank and acknowledge Antonette Baretto, Annie Markowitz, and Jenny Wong, who facilitated the completion of this manual. Many thanks also to Bobbe Needham for her thoughtful, considered, and sensitive work on the manuscript.

We also want to recognize and appreciate the tutors who have worked with tutees and contributed their field notes, interest, and imagination to this manual, and the teachers and administrators who welcomed them into their classrooms and tutoring centers over the past few years. We thank the many concerned teachers and administrators who worked with us to provide the tutoring sites, especially Lucia Diaz, Risa Getchman, Morgan P. Hatch, Jr., Gloria Martinez, and Sharmen C. Taylor. We also acknowledge the hard work of Cynthia Chavez, who along with Nima Fahimian was the first tutoring coordinator. They were supported from the office of Parvin Kassie, Field Studies, UCLA. Excellent coordination was continued by Makhameh Maggie Kharrazi, Tiffany Hamilton, Seina Takamatsu, and Roger (Sung Gon) Kim.

We thank all the students from the Sociology of Education course who shared their time with tutees and whose experiences with those tutees enriched the class and everyone else's tutoring experiences. We have tried here to personally acknowledge the tutors who specifically contributed to this manual—any omissions are the fault of incomplete records. Thanks to Janet Abronson, Jacob Ahdoot, Adelaida Alfiler, Chantelle Ameli, Elizabeth Antunez, Allison Appleby, John Aquino, Laura Aquino, Anita Avalos, Kecia Ayabe, Eliazer Ayala, Bobby Babai, Esmeralda Barajas, Thomas Barnes, Mary Barr, Jovy-Marie Bayani, Vivian Benitez, Kimberly Berg, Nina Bermudez, Marie Botello, Ashley Braband, Nikki Brinton, Bernadette Bullock, Kim Broadbeck, Eleyna Byington, Darren Capeloto, Tarek Captan, Jennifer Carmel, John Catetti, Lori Chang, Jessica Chavez, Lisa Chinn, Ahra Cho, Hee-Jin Choi, Rose Chung, Deatra Clinton, Veronica Contreras, Maha Dakhil, Marianne de Francia, Lakan de Leon, Yusef Daulatzai, Laurel Davis, Zalika Davis, Dianne Dizon, Andrea Duncan, Trisha Elegino (TRE), Ernso Ermo, Donna Estacio, Wendy Estevez, Tina Farris, Jennifer Fields, Anthony Fong, Rafael Gaeta, Juana Garcia, Jessica Gawitt, Brenda Generazio, Guelsy Gomez, Maricela Gomez, Minerva Gomez, Marianne Gomis, Paulina Gonzalez, Sara Gonzales, Andre Grissette, Antonia Guerrero, Elena Guerrero, Araceli Gutierrez, Rene Haloossim, Simon Hamlin, Tiffany Hamilton, Vanessa Hartstrom, Sandra Harvey, Michael Haskell, Justine Henry, Belinda Hernandez, Marisela Hernandez, Jasmine Hines, Aiyana Holm, LaShell Holton, Joyce Hu, Suzanna Huesca, Trang Hugnh, Teresa Hui, Kimberley Ingram, Milaine Isaac, Jennifer Jung, Jennifer Kane, Ani Karayan, Hanie Kim, Jessica Kim, Joy Kim, Roger Kim, Young-Ki Kim, Gloria King, Patra Kittichanthira, Elizabeth Kyriacou, Claire Lagao, Christine LeBard, Teresa Lanz, Edna Lopez, Oralia Lua, Elsa Luna, Howana Lundy, Shawn Mai, Sandra Margulies, Scott Markham, Colleen Martich, Lisa Martinelli, Denise Martinez, Thelma Martinez, Brady Matoian,

Rebecca McConnell, Kendra Melendez, Joshua Mendelsohn, Deborah Mendoza, Tesz Millan, Jennifer Mickey, Erika Miller, Sylvia Miravet, Scott Mitchell, Christina Montanez, Billie Monzon, Natasha Moradi, Cheryl Morris, Maya Muneno, Christian Munguia, LeBaron Myers, Kevin Nakahara, Nazanin Nassir, Nga Nguy, Justine Nguyen, Christina Nunez, Ijeoma Odu, Eddie Palm, Pamela Park, Leah Pate, Hope Penkala, Rachelle Pensanti, Kelly Petriccione, Darcy Purdy, Natalie Rayes, Lucia Reyes, Vashira Rhodes, Tammy Richardson, Maisha Riddlesprigger, Teresa Robles, Yanitza Rodriguez, Jonathan Rosales, Roselma Samala, Edith Sanchez, Michael Schwartz, Donovan Seno, Angela Seo, Kana Shahabi, Angel Sim, Paula Smith, Joseph Simbillo, Natalie Soohoo, Linda Steele, Branda Stewart, Jocelyn Su, Jenny Sugimura, Brian Suitzer, Kevin Sved, Nicole Swan, Margaret Swift, Nancy Takahashi, Seina Takamatsu, Paulino Tamayo, Polly Tattersall, Tricia Taylor, Jacki Tenerelli, Tara Topper, Karla Torres, Olga Torres, Sigrin Torres, Dinh Tran, Huy Tran, Aarin Ulrich, Joanne Valencia, Priscilla Veres, Yvette Villalobos, Brian Waldman, Chelsea Walsh, Jocelyn Wang, Lisa Ward, Alicia Way, Ben Weitz, Ryan Welsh, Grace Wen, Terri Wong, Amy Wood, Katrin Yadgari, Allison Yen, Mitsue Yokota, Duk Yoon, Joy Yoshikawa, Kevin Yuen, and Margarita Zepeda.

Finally, we wish to acknowledge the contributions that all of our tutees have made, both to the education of UCLA students and to this book. As a way of returning part of what they have given us, a portion of all royalties from this book will be given to the UCLA Field Studies Program for its continuing support of experiential education.

Introduction

If you listen to the political rhetoric, tutoring has become the great solution to America's social problems. The Bushes, the Gores, and the Clintons all talk tutoring, and even California's Republican former governor, Pete Wilson, is a mentor—it is the average citizen's way to help to make this country a village. Corporations are enjoined to adopt inner-city schools, giving executives a chance to mentor and serve as role models for children who might otherwise know no life other than the streets. University students are urged to go out into their communities and volunteer in schools, with immigrants, or with programs designed to eliminate adult illiteracy. And it makes perfect sense. Why shouldn't those with greater financial and educational resources try to help those shortchanged by public schools or struggling to survive in this nation without spoken and written English skills?

The opportunities are endless. To find a place to volunteer in the Los Angeles area, one must only open the *Los Angeles Times* to the "Involvement Opportunities" column to find several tutoring sites a week. The *Times* also runs frequent features on exemplary mentoring or tutoring programs in the city. On a smaller scale, you can't walk the paths of UCLA without being confronted, either by people or flyers, with a multitude of tutoring programs, and we imagine that other college campuses have similar programs.

The question then is, Why isn't everyone tutoring? Almost

everyone will admit that it sounds like a good idea (it doesn't take tax dollars, and it gives everyday citizens a chance to do something personally), the number of people tutoring still doesn't match the hype. We think the answer may be found in a conversation one of us overheard one day on Bruin Walk, UCLA's main drag and home base for most the campus's philanthropy booths. Two girls walking together paused to take a blue flyer for Bruin Partners, a program that buses UCLA students to an inner-city elementary school once a week for one-on-one tutoring.

"I'd really like to do that."

"Yeah, me too. But how do you think you do it?"

"I don't know—that's the problem. I don't know if I'd *know* how to do it."

The girls then carefully folded their blue flyers into neat squares and tucked them into their backpacks, surely meaning to look at them later. But they probably never called the number on the flyers, not because they didn't want to tutor, but because they were unsure. Is it right to sign up for something, especially something important, if you don't know what you're doing?

It's a significant question. Why would the average executive expect to be able to relate to inner-city elementary school students? Or, perhaps more poignantly, how could nineteen-year-old university students hope to teach a forty-year-old immigrant with more life experience than they can imagine? Tutoring is supposed to be the great equalizer, and it can be. But it doesn't always look that way on the surface. And it's the surface that scares people away.

No matter how many times you've tutored, and no matter how confident you are in your ability to teach, walking into a new site always seems to bring back the same vague question: Isn't anyone going to show me how to do this? Usually no one does. The assumption is that, if you have more education than your students and the will to teach, you can do it. And you can. But that doesn't mean that you know how to—or that you have the confidence to try.

After years of tutoring and of sending students out to tutor, we are acutely aware of how much this book is needed. It would have been so much easier for those girls on Bruin Walk to get involved in tutoring, to call the number on the blue flyer, if they had only felt that they knew what they were doing. The people that our leaders are calling upon to tutor are people who are competent in their lives—professionals, university students, people successful in their fields *because* they know what they are doing and hesitate to enter situations in which they don't.

We hope, with this book, to make it possible for you to feel as confident and successful at tutoring as you do in the other aspects of your life. If you are interested in helping another to learn, this book will guide you. We have tried to develop a set of principles that will help you through this very intricate process. All of you have tutored before, of course. As parents or relatives, you have taught a child to hike a ball, make cookies, play chess, iron clothes, or write letters. As students, you have taught your peers or your siblings how to work through math problems or understand complicated lectures. You have done all this without self-consciousness or anxiety, and tutoring can work in much the same way. Your tutees' natural curiosity, interest, and desire to please you, perhaps even to be like you, usually ensure that your tutoring will succeed.

But a parent, relative, peer, or sibling generally does not have to confront the different styles of learning and differences in class, race, ethnicity, and religion that are often present in tutoring situations. Parents and students are not necessarily educated in how to keep tutee *learning* in the forefront. Tutoring draws on our natural abilities to teach and explain, but it is also a unique situation that calls for new attitudes and adjustments.

Tutoring requires the tutor to realize that learning enriches the whole student—mind, motivation, curiosity. Many people still believe that grades and Scholastic Assessment Test (SAT), Law

School Admissions Test (LSAT), and Medical College Admissions Test (MCAT) scores represent intelligence. This idea emphasizes student memorization for tests rather than deliberate thought aimed at solving puzzles or problems. Intelligence is more a matter of seeing what we do with the *unknown* than memorizing and dealing with what we *already know*. Tutors can do what teachers and parents often cannot manage: they can be patient, taking the time to observe, question, support, challenge, and applaud. They can move toward nurturing the true and total intelligence of their tutees.

In this spirit, we offer you this manual. We believe that the practice and understanding of the tutoring process will start you on a journey that begins when you confront your own experiences, biases, and beliefs. It ends when your tutees know that they are special, that they matter, that they can undertake their own learning with a degree of self-confidence, that they can take risks and fail at times (all of us fail, and failure is necessary for learning).

In tutoring them, you can help your students face the world and others with openness and confidence. And in the end, you gain even more than your tutee, because you will have made a difference in someone's life.

There is much talk in our country about helping others: the poor, the weak, the "other Americans." The belief that others need us because they are deficient in some way does a great disservice to both tutor and tutee. We encourage tutors, instead of harboring this view, to see that tutoring allows the tutor an opportunity to learn—about patience, the power of affirmation, and acceptance. We believe that this book offers the chance for tutors to help themselves, probably even more than they help the "other."

In this time of consumerism, materialism, diminishing support for public education and struggling teachers, endless debates on pedagogical style, busing, school choice vouchers, and bilingual education, this manual cuts through to what is most important: the students' learning. Wherever the political winds blow, our book will work. Whatever the subjects of intellectual debates, this book will work. It will work for you and your tutee because it is based on the importance of caring, respectful human contact.

It seems strange that a book like this wasn't written long ago. But the inherent problem in teaching people to tutor is that every tutoring scenario is different. Tutoring is based on an individual relationship—how can a book address every one of those? Everyone approaches relationships and tutoring differently, so how can one person, or even a few people, hope to convey the unique character of tutoring in one general manual?

The beauty of this book is that in it you won't find just a few people talking to you, just one professor's teaching ideology, or a couple of people's success stories. This manual was not simply written; the ideas contained in it were not simply conjured up by someone sitting at a desk. They grew. We have talked with and read the field notes of hundreds of tutors, and through these interactions we got a sense of how they built relationships with their students, what their successes were, and how they adjusted and improved their teaching. We've looked at the experiences of tutors and tutees of many nationalities and ethnicities, of all races, of most religions and of degrees of religiosity from orthodox to none at all, and of all sexual orientations and social classes. Over the years, our feelings, intuitions, and hunches have been either confirmed or changed, based on the actual experiences of real tutors. It is this consensus that we have put together for you.

A technical note: we have changed all the names of tutees and of tutors to preserve their anonymity.

Of course, we can't prescribe any one right way to tutor. Instead, we lay out a number of guidelines for building a tutoring relationship and teaching your student. You don't have to take our advice on blind faith. You will hear the voices of the tutors that we have learned from, so that you can bring the wealth and wisdom of their experience into your own work. We hope that from this base, you can build invaluable and unforgettable tutoring experiences, for both you and your tutees.

Recommended Reading

In *Ten Promising Programs for Educating All Children: Evidence of Impact* (1997), Rebecca Herman and Sam Stringfield evaluate ten types of teaching models. Their study is a particularly useful one for teachers, as it discusses promising school programs and the barriers to them. These programs not only have succeeded in improving students' reading, math, and language scores, but have been accompanied by a decline in absences, suspensions, and corporal punishment. One of the successful models that the authors describe, operating in more than 600 schools, has a tutorial component in which tutors meet three times a week with tutees, who are at least one year behind grade level. Such models offer suggestions as to how tutoring might be incorporated in other classrooms.

Although the fieldwork for this manual derives mostly from tutors whose tutees are children, a significant number of the examples come from the experience of tutors working with high school students and adults. A number of empirical studies have looked at programs for tutees of different ages, at how successful tutoring can be, and at how different tutoring models work. For a start, see *Schooling Disadvantaged Children: Racing against Catastrophe* (1990), in which Gary Natriello, Edward L. McDill, and Aaron M. Pallas present a review of studies of the effects of tutoring programs for disadvantaged students. In "Educational Outcomes of Tutoring: A Meta-analysis of Findings" (1982), Peter A. Cohn, James A. Kulick, and Chen-Lin Kulick lay out a meta-analysis of sixty-five studies of peer tutoring. They find that children who are tutored outperform those who receive no tutoring on two levels: subject matter and positive attitudes toward schoolwork. They also find that even short periods of tutoring can have a positive impact on children.

1
Attitudes, Anxieties, and Expectations

Fear and anxiety are natural emotions we often feel in our daily encounters and interactions with others. New situations such as tutoring, where people start out as strangers, frequently heighten these feelings. Tutoring is not just any new situation, however; the great challenges, expectations, and social complications it brings compound normal fears and anxieties. When recounting their first days in the classroom, even veteran educators report feelings similar to those experienced by the following new tutor:

> I was extremely nervous, since I was not very sure if the kids would like me. I felt a great deal of pressure, since I had never tutored in my life. I thought I could not offer the children anything, because I was questioning my abilities to teach. In addition, would the teacher like me? Would I get along with her? Then, scared and intimidated by the size and the beauty of the school, I did not know if I should turn back and run, or walk into the supervisor's office with confidence and integrity.

Even if such anxious feelings subside after the first day, as the setting becomes somewhat familiar and the tutor-tutee relationship gets underway, new fears arise throughout the tutoring experience. Fear, anxiety, and insecurity are intrinsic to tutoring. Intricate situations and emotionally taxing incidents can make tutors feel not only helpless, but even a threat to the educational progress of their tutees. As complicated and discouraging as such feelings may be, your knowledge and application of certain governing attitudes and practices will equip you with some basic methods of dealing with both first-day and ongoing problems and concerns.

Because many tutors share the same *fears and anxieties*, we have found a set of general *attitudes and practices* that, when brought into the tutoring scenario, can ease these concerns. The most common fears that new tutors express surface in such questions as Will my student like me? Will I like my new student? Will I be able to fit in and relate to a student who is very different from me (in terms of gender, age, race, ethnicity, religion, or socioeconomic status)? Will I be able to teach everything that there is to be taught? Will I succeed as a tutor?

Such questions are not only common, they are reasonable for anyone entering a new or unfamiliar tutoring situation. But they need not be paralyzing. In spite of your fears and anxieties, rewarding experiences will emerge once you have made a connection with your tutee. When your tutees realize that you tutor because you care and that you are genuinely interested in them and in having a strong tutor-tutee bond, tutoring becomes an experience filled with moments of pleasure, satisfaction, and joy, and your fears and anxieties recede. Tutors often come out of their tutoring relationships with a much deeper sense of satisfaction than they had expected. Reactions often include such sentiments as "I got so much more than I offered," "He'll never know how much he affected me," and "I found this experience to be the most important thing I've ever done."

We have found that most successful tutoring partnerships spring from a common underlying concept: *unconditional acceptance*. Unconditional acceptance is the basis for the set of attitudes and practices we discuss throughout this chapter. It is also the most basic and essential foundation for a strong, successful tutoring relationship.

One of the best ways to overcome or at least dilute your fears and anxieties is to try to ground yourself in unconditional acceptance as you enter your tutoring scenario. The first step in doing this is to adopt a certain set of *attitudes* before entering and while engaging in the tutoring situation. These attitudes can both ease tutors' fears and shape tutors into better and more open teachers. The essential attitudes for tutoring, all flowing from unconditional acceptance, involve *giving up expectations*, *displaying enthusiasm and interest*, and *feeling empathy*.

These components not only help develop a suitable and successful tutoring mindset, but they lay the foundation for a number of effective tutoring *practices*. We have found three general practices very useful in creating a comfortable and successful tutoring relationship: *being patient*, *being observant and asking questions*, and *understanding students on their own level*.

Normal Fears and Anxieties

The good news is that most tutors overcome their initial fears and anxieties about tutoring. Knowing what to expect, and knowing that most of your fellow tutors have felt the same concerns, may alleviate your anxieties. Tutoring is not easy; it will constantly confront you with your own weaknesses and failings. This can be difficult for anyone. For one who has just committed to helping others, it can be devastating. But because *almost every tutor* experiences these feelings, almost every successful tutor has had to overcome them.

Will the Students Like Me?

Many new tutors are concerned with whether or not their assigned student will like them. Will the tutee accept them as a friend and a role model? As a white female tutor reflects on her experience, she expresses a general concern of many tutors: "Although I do like children, I do not know that I am very approachable, for some reason. Maybe it is because I do not have much contact with children in my daily activities, I suppose I am not quite used to being around them nor know how to treat them or at least do not have much experience in doing so."

Like this tutor, many worry that they will not be compatible either with children in general or with their specifically assigned tutee. Besides worrying about how kids will react to their personalities, tutors also worry about how tutees will see them, what first impressions they may have. Tutors are often afraid that they will not look like the type of person the tutee will want to work with.

Most tutors wake up on the morning of their first day of tutoring anxious over what to wear, how to comb their hair, and how they look overall. One male tutor writes, "Maybe I would be looked up to as a big brother, or maybe because of my six-foot three-inch stature they would be afraid of me."

Will I Like My Students?

Tangential to the previous concern is whether or not you will like the students to whom you have been assigned. What if a child is obnoxious or completely unmotivated? What if a tutee doesn't want to be there or deliberately asks things that you can't answer and makes tutoring difficult for you?

Whenever you are assigned to spend a lot of time with someone whom you don't know, it's natural to wonder if you'll get along. And obviously, if you've been assigned to help them, it's normal to wonder if you'll really want to once you get to know them.

Will I Be Able to Fit in with and Understand Kids Who Are Different?

In tutoring, differences between tutors and tutees are a very big concern, especially because tutors and tutees often come from very different backgrounds. It is to many tutors' credit that they are concerned with and interested in working through these differences, but their enormity may scare some tutors away. Is it possible for an upper-middle-class white university student or business executive to form a close relationship with a young African American student from the inner city? Can a female tutor from a sheltered background ever hope to relate to a street-tough gang member? It's easy to wonder. And since people often interact with a rather homogeneous group of people in their everyday lives, the idea of tutoring "other" types of people is often intimidating.

Even tutors who are confident that they can form a relationship with a student from a different background sometimes worry that they won't be an appropriate role model for someone who may have to face radically different life experiences than they themselves have ever known. This occurred to one white female student at a nonprofit community outreach program in Los Angeles that works to empower minority children (mostly African Americans, with some Latino students).

> At the beginning it was very difficult. I had many fears and wondered how I could possibly make an impact on anyone's life. I kept questioning why these minority children would look up to an upper-middle-class white person who is almost their own age. In addition, I also questioned how I would fit into the environment and become involved in the things the children and the program are taking part in. What do I know about the South Central community anyway? I mean, I am an outsider here. How do I become an insider, and am I even supposed to?

Will I Be Able to Teach the Students?

In addition to wondering if forming a relationship is possible, many tutorss worry about their teaching competence. In fact, even when tutors find that they are immediately accepted and put at ease by the students they have been assigned to tutor, the issue of how well they will teach still lingers, as in the following example. This female tutor was welcomed into the fourth-grade classroom to which she was assigned, yet she was still nervous about being an effective teacher.

> A perceptive boy named Roger from the front of the room yelled out, "Hey, are you one of the tutors from UCLA?" When I confirmed Roger's question with a nod, smiles spread throughout the room. Two girls seated near me shyly asked, "Can we work with you today?" This was my first experience in the classroom, and it felt wonderful. I was really nervous because I felt the children looked up to me and expected me to know all of the answers, since I was a big college student. I was also nervous because I was afraid that the children wouldn't be interested in working, but only talking. I wasn't sure how I would be able to focus their attention or motivate them to learn.

Maybe you've never taught before. Maybe you're shaky in a couple of subjects. Tutoring tends to exacerbate insecurities about a tutor's own academic performance. Many tutors find themselves driving to their tutoring site trying to figure out how they will tell a student that they have never been good in math themselves.

Many factors may contribute to tutors' evaluations of their own ability. Often their personal expectations when they become tutors lead them to self-doubt and force them to question their teaching abilities and techniques. As one tutor explains: "Inadequacy is a very hard pill to swallow. I felt disappointed in myself, depressed and defeated. What if they need help with math and I cannot remember? I never did well in math. What if I cannot come up with innovative and fun ways of teaching?"

Will I Succeed?

Most people get into tutoring because they want to make a difference in another person's life, but motivations for tutoring vary. Perhaps it's required in a class you're taking. Perhaps you were inspired by a newspaper or television show. Maybe you are trying to make a political or social statement. No matter why they decide to tutor, most tutors have some idea of what they want to accomplish—and usually it's the betterment of their students. But what if the students won't listen? What if they still fail all their tests? What if they go out and get arrested the day after you have a heart-to-heart in a tutoring session? The aftermath of many tutoring situations may look like failure, and many tutors fear that they might have been part of the cause.

One of the amazing things about tutoring is just how overpowering these fears can seem. What's more amazing is how often they are overcome, and that, in the end, it is usually the tutee's calming effect that helps a tutor's fears disappear. As one tutor explained: "When I saw the fondness in this little girl's eyes, I realized that I have to let go of my insecurities and occupy my time thinking of ways I can provide these kids with techniques for learning."

As this quote suggests, many of the normal worries and anxieties you may feel as you enter your tutoring site will disappear once you meet your tutee. Most of your fears will vanish when you find a real-life tutee before you. Yet there are ways to approach a tutoring situation that will minimize your worries and fears and often help you overcome them.

Unconditional Acceptance

Unconditional acceptance means accepting other people, suspending any hopes or expectations of what you would like them to be. When we accept people unconditionally, it is not because they gratify us or make us proud of their accomplishments, not because they win races or spelling contests. It is because of who they are. Although this emotion usually develops over time with family and friends, you don't have that kind of time in a tutoring situation. That's why it's important to cultivate this accepting attitude before you enter the tutoring relationship.

You admire a flower for its color, its height, its petals. You love it not because it complements your decor, or because it complements you, your clothes, or other flowers, or requires little water or little sun, or lots of water and lots of sun. You admire and love it for what it is, and you accept it for what it is, apart from your needs, desires, hopes, expectations, or fears. Think of your tutee as a flower. Although tutoring will often leave you feeling wonderful, tutoring does not exist for you, your ego, or your fulfillment. It exists for the students, and toward that aim you need to accept them for whomever they are. Unconditional acceptance is an ideal, a lofty goal we will often fall short of, but one we can strive for.

This ideal comprises a set of attitudes and practices that become apparent in the example that follows. For this volunteer tutor who works with a different child every week at a children's hospital, all days are first days, and first days are often the most fear filled of the tutoring experience. Although this tutor met much more challenging conditions than those many tutors encounter, the issues raised are typical of every tutoring situation. Brandon's case illustrates that, regardless of the challenges awaiting a tutor on the first day, there is always the possibility of creating a bond.

I met Brandon, a seven-year-old liver transplant patient. Brandon seemed frail and very indifferent to his surroundings. He refused to communicate with the nurse in words and only pointed to things if he needed anything.

"Hi, Brandon, my name is Tim, and I am here to spend some time with you."

No response, not even a nod or look toward my way.

The nurse interjected, "Brandon, isn't this great—we have a volunteer to play with you."

He continued watching the TV as if he couldn't care less about anything that was happening.

"Brandon, would you like to go to the playroom?"

He shook his head from side to side without looking at me.

"Would you like me to bring you a game or video?"

Same response.

Frustrated, I looked around, feeling like a fool, while fighting the thoughts in my head, "You may be making him uncomfortable. He doesn't like you. Maybe he wants to be left alone. Maybe I should explain to him that I am not a physician or a nurse. What is he thinking? I feel useless. He likes animals, especially dinosaurs and reptiles. Look at his shelf, filled with gifts that had one theme in common: dinosaurs, monsters, and jungles."

I left the room without saying a word. On my way to the storage room, I ordered for him the King Kong Nintendo game. From the storage room I fetched a game called Dynamite (a dinosaur game, in which whoever gets to the finish line first, after going through a jungle full of obstacles, wins). Being insecure in my choice of the game, I also grabbed Battleship. I walked quietly to his room, carrying the games in my hand. I did not announce my entrance, much less the games that I fetched him.

I didn't need to, because he snapped out of his bed and snatched Dynamite with an unfriendly gesture.

While he opened the box and seemingly read the instructions, I sat next to him on his bed, without asking him. He did not object, but instead set up the game and chose his green dinosaur. I chose the yellow one, while he tossed the dice.

Brandon breezed through the game, reading the cards silently. I was flabbergasted at his quickness. Needless to say, he beat me, and I didn't even try to give him the game. While the game was going on I asked him questions about the moves, but he refused to utter a word or even make the smallest noise, he only pointed to things. His refusal to talk continued even when the Nintendo game arrived and I was desperately searching for an electrical outlet. He did finally point to a corner of a room where I finally found one after three minutes of searching.

I had to wonder, "Wasn't he excited about the game? Doesn't he want to get started as early as possible considering the short amount of time we have the game in reserve?"

He hooked up the system. Then, he gave me the other joystick for no apparent reason, since he set the game on the "one player" mode and kept on playing the next ten games, while I watched and commented on what I thought was cool about the game. Then, suddenly, he handed me his joystick.

So I entered one of the houses, but soon dropped off of a cliff and died. Apparently the route I took was a difficult one. Brandon knew that, but obviously preferred not to tell me in words. After I died, he took a joystick from my hand, entered the same route, and threw himself off the cliff on purpose. Then, he looked at me and handed me the joystick.

So Brandon did tell me about the dangers of the path I took, but he did in his own terms, implying that I should change the route. He was willing to lose the two of the monkeys that he had saved over the past ten games with so much effort rather than tell me in words, "Do not follow that path." This was a rich gesture full of meaning to me.

At this point, I started doubting his ability to speak English, or to speak anything, period. But to me the gesture showed care and concern. He lost two of his men to guide me—he sacrificed for me!

As he got tired with the game, his mother called on the phone. Lo and behold he was talking to his mother in perfect English—once again making me feel foolish. So much for my language theory.

When he needed help to go to the bathroom, after the phone call, he suggested by pointing down, and pointing to whatever he needed. I could not understand what he needed for awhile, and he kept pointing till I got it; he preferred to withstand the push on his bladder but not to speak a word to me.

Our session ended with his last interest of the day: making race cars using Legos. The box to which he was pointing noted "ages 8–12." However, for this seven year old, with his right arm in a cast and problematic physical conditions, putting together the race car was a matter of minutes—a task that would take me at least ten minutes. When I tried to help, he took the pieces from my hand and was rather eager to show off what he was capable of doing.

When he was done, I said goodbye and thanked him for a fun time.

This tutor's experience demonstrates that even with the most recalcitrant tutee, a persistent tutor can make a connection. Although this is the type of situation that most tutors would prefer not to encounter on their first day, we have identified a number of attitudes and practices that should help ease your way, whatever the circumstances.

Attitudes

Developing an attitude of unconditional acceptance involves *giving up expectations, showing enthusiasm and interest,* and *feeling empathy.* These are the most general, fundamental elements in initiating a positive tutoring experience; they lay the foundation for successful tutoring practices.

Although it may be hard to imagine developing your attitudes toward tutoring before you even reach the site, it's worth your time to give it some thought. Some tutoring sites allow you time to acclimate yourself and get to know the students and staff, but there are times when tutors are immediately matched up with students—before you even know what's going on, you're tutoring. So it's useful to have already established some sort of mindset.

As you will see, beginning to work out your mindset and attitudes before you begin tutoring does *not* mean you should try to figure out your teaching techniques and goals for your student in advance. As each tutoring scenario is different and tutees generally will not conform to your expectations, such preparation would be a waste of time, even detrimental. But there is still mental preparation that you can do. Before you reach the site, you can *give up any expectations* that you may have, and you can work toward orienting yourself to the positive emotions of *enthusiasm, interest,* and *empathy.*

GIVING UP EXPECTATIONS
Start out with minimal expectations. This means giving up visions of what you expect or hope to see happen and what you think you will know and feel or not know and not feel. Expectations that tutors cannot give up can cause tension in the tutoring session. When such expectations are not met (which is usually the case), the tutor can become disillusioned and disheartened, emotions that can harm the relationship.

Our expectations are constructed through our value systems, upbringing, and past experiences and can be very different from those of others. These expectations can become major sources of frustration when not met or matched by others' behavior, such as that of our tutees.

The best thing to do is to try to enter tutoring without any expectations at all. This, of course, includes giving up expectations you may have of your future students and their personalities, their academic skills or progress, and their motivation and attitude toward you. Every child is different. They have different backgrounds, different strengths, and different weaknesses. Some may be thrilled to be tutored; others may be suspicious. A tutor's conception of a student should be a blank slate. Tutors must be prepared to accept and work with any student they are assigned.

Giving up expectations of how a tutee is supposed to act or be does not, however, preclude your holding high expectations for your tutees' educational potential. It does not mean that you should not at all times challenge your tutees to work as hard as they can and to excel. Tutors need to form, *through tutoring*, a picture or an image of where they would like their individual tutees to move educationally. (This kind of informed, or *educated, expectations* we will address later.)

But giving up expectations applies to far more than your tutee. It means giving up expectations of yourself. It means giving up expectations of the school system, the teachers, and tutoring in general. It means giving up expectations of success.

Every tutor can help a child, but no tutor is superhuman. You cannot expect to know everything or to know how to teach everything. And every tutoring partnership can be a success, but not all tutees will land a scholarship to Harvard. Big successes are wonderful, but so are little successes. In fact, little successes make up the bulk of a successful tutoring relationship. Every tutor can make an impact on a child, and any positive impact you make is a success. It is up to the individuals involved in the relationship to determine just what the successes will be.

Giving up expectations is hard. When you make a commitment to tutor, it's difficult not to start thinking about what you will be dealing with and trying to prepare yourself mentally and emotionally. But as you can see, shedding your expectations will also help you shed many of your fears. *Will you be able to teach?* Of course. You may not know everything, but you aren't expected to. Being rusty in trigonometry doesn't make you a bad tutor. Not knowing Spanish does not make it impossible to relate to a Spanish-only-speaking child. You will be perfectly capable of teaching many subjects, and beyond helping with schoolwork, every tutor can teach students about motivation and hard work, about enjoying learning, and simply that there are teachers who care. It's comforting to remember that an adult merely being there and working with children can help improve their comprehension and vocabulary.

Forgive yourself if you don't live up to how you want to teach. The tutor in the example that follows, a Persian female who seemed a perfect match for her Farsi-speaking third-grade student, found forgiving herself difficult; she ended a session extremely frustrated with herself.

I asked Ahmed what he wanted to do and he said, "Let's study English." I was surprised, considering he had not done such a good job last time around. However, this time around, instead of asking him for the other letters in the alphabet, I went straight after the letter "M" [which had been troublesome for him in previous sessions]. I could not believe my own two eyes when I saw that blank look on his face. I thought to myself, "How stupid can someone be? I don't understand. What am I doing wrong?"

I hesitated to help him. Instead of helping him, I decided that we will sit there for as long as it takes, until he remembers the letter "M." Little did I know that we were going to sit there for a long time. I started to give him hints, pronouncing words that start with the letter "M." However, he still did not know what I was talking about. I told him to write down whatever he thinks looks like "M." He wrote the letter "N" instead.

When I looked at him, he was playing with his fingers. I could not believe it. I was furious. In an angry, yet strong tone of voice, I snapped at him. He jumped out of his chair. Tears were circling his eyes. He looked at me as though I had just hit him or something. I felt really bad. I kept on apologizing, but it was not good enough. From that moment on, he would just look at me. Not that he talked much before, now he did not even say a single word.

I tried to make it up to him, but I guess it was useless. I calmed myself down and wrote the letter "M" on the piece of paper in front of him. He stared at it for a bit and then started to write the letter "M" until the last line of the paper. I focused his attention on other letters, and when I got back to the letter "M," surprisingly enough, he remembered. He had a smile on his face.

I cannot make any excuses for my behavior. All I can say is that I was very frustrated by the fact that we had spent the entire past two weeks studying the letter "M." I also know that this is no excuse to snap at a child. I wish he knew how sorry I am.

This incident, while not ideal as far as tutoring methods go, is an excellent instance of a tutor getting upset with herself and her teaching skills. It shows how tutor expectations of how quickly a child can learn, and how well tutors should teach, can fill a situation with tension. The important thing to remember is that even though Aaron's tutor was not at her best in this situation, he forgave her, and he was still able to learn. You must try to be as forgiving with yourself.

Like Ahmed and his tutor, allow your tutees to help teach you how to teach! Teaching someone an idea, concept, or skill can be extremely challenging, especially when you "just know" how to do it. You'll find that many skills you have to teach are ones that you learned through rote memorization. Finding more constructive and creative ways to teach these same skills can be difficult, but here you and your tutee have the most to learn from one another.

Will you be able to succeed? Again, forget your notions of what constitutes success. Success is different for everyone. Every tutoring scenario, regardless of the caliber of either the student or the tutor as a teacher, can be a success.

More than allowing you to calm some of your fears, approaching tutoring situations with no expectations lets you view the scene more clearly. Your lenses—that is, your expectations—do not cloud or color what is going on. Looking back at the hospital incident, one can see that what the medical volunteer expected from his interaction with Brandon was bound to defeat him had he not relaxed and dismissed it.

Unconditional acceptance of your tutee means dismissing your preconceived notions about how your tutee should react toward you and learn from you. In the following example, a straight female tutor working at a gay and lesbian center was terrified by her own expectations:

At first I was worried that my intentions for tutoring at a gay and lesbian after-school program would be misunderstood and questioned by the students. I am heterosexual and was afraid that they may think I am tutoring at the center because I was homosexual myself. I was also afraid that once they found out they might not let me into their lives and accept me. I guess I was projecting. My preconceived notions of how it would be were momentarily confirmed by a question that my female tutee [17-year-old Latina] asked me on the first day: "Do you have a boyfriend?"

This question threw me off balance. I was shocked that she asked me such a question right away; I knew that she was trying to find out about whether I belonged to her world.

Hesitantly, expecting a cold reaction, I said, "Yes." To my surprise the answer didn't seem to change her behavior. Instead she went on telling me about how every time she gets into a fight with her girlfriend, her parents use it against her homosexual relationship. Then relating to me she asked, "Don't you and your boyfriend have major disagreements?" Embarrassed about my shaky and obviously nervous reactions toward her, I said "Yes" and explained to her an incident I had with my boyfriend.

This tutor's preoccupation and anxiety sprang from her own fears and misconceptions about homosexuals. Her expectations not only made her nervous, they could have damaged her relationship with the tutee from the very beginning. *Can you get along with a tutee who is different from you?* Can you make a connection? Yes, you can, but you must be willing to give up your preconceived notions and accept your tutee unconditionally.

In the following example a white male tutor reflects upon a tutoring partnership in which he and the tutee came from dramatically different ethnic, religious, and class backgrounds. The tutor was raised in an upper-middle-class, strict Jewish household; the tutee, a seven-year-old Latina, came from a working-class background. This tutor eventually came to realize that his preconceived notions kept the two of them from forming a relationship for several weeks.

I was assigned to tutor Marta, a second-grade Latina, who came from a family with low socioeconomic status. As a university tutor I was confident about being able to help my tutee with any problems she may have. But ironically the problem was my inability to immerse myself in her life, and see her problems, and perceive her actions in the context of her surroundings. I was so preoccupied with how I would affect her life the way I had learned how to and teaching her from my experiences that I ignored the greater problems in Marta's life. She seemed "impossible" to teach, and focus . . . I could see that she did not identify with me and really ignored my concerns. It took me a while to realize that I could not expect her to understand my concerns because they were so foreign and irrelevant to her life.

I didn't find out about her mother physically beating her, her teacher yelling at her in class, and the students in the bus calling her "stupid," until the sixth week of tutoring, once I finally learned *how to listen*. Once deemed deserving of a pass into her world, we learned to grow together and learn from one another, by putting things in the context of our lives.

As we will see later, once the lens of expectations is removed, you will be able to make important observations about your tutees that will allow you to better understand their world. Your careful observations should enable you to connect with your tutees and the world that impacts their lives, to approach and interact with them on their own terms. If you make no or few judgments beforehand, it's possible to experience what it is to live in their world, even if it is completely foreign to you.

Going back to the hospital example, we can see that once the volunteer gave up his expectations regarding Brandon's lack of communication and lack of enthusiasm toward the volunteer's presence, the volunteer could focus on Brandon's surroundings and seek some way to approach him. The environmental cues, such as toys and books surrounding Brandon's bed, enabled the volunteer to fetch a game involving dinosaurs that was naturally exciting for the boy. Through this technique, the volunteer was also able express his interest and enthusiasm for interacting with Brandon, for he paid attention to what Brandon enjoyed doing.

DISPLAYING ENTHUSIASM AND INTEREST

It is crucial that you show your passion for tutoring by showing interest in your students' work and in their lives. Children can see right through you, and the care you show for your work—your tutoring—will translate into love and care for your tutees. Tutees know that you cannot start loving them right away (human relationships do not operate that way), but your obvious love for your work and interest in them will illustrate your potential for bonding with them.

Don't worry about *whether or not a student will like you*. Students will be able to tell if you are genuinely interested in them and in your work, and their impressions of you will flow from that perception. Whether they immediately like your personality or the way you look is unimportant. What is important is that they understand that you are someone who cares for them and about them, and that it is safe for them to respond to your desire to form a relationship.

Furthermore, by showing your enthusiasm and interest, you demonstrate your flexibility and ability to meet them on their terms. Many adults fail to do this when they interact with children or with anyone whom they are helping. Because your tutees have often been denied passion and enthusiasm from adults, they may at first see you as just another authority figure. As a result, they will often test you a few times. They're checking your sincerity. The only way to prove that you are trustworthy is to show sincere and open interest in them and what they are doing.

The tutor in the following example was not received with any enthusiasm by the tutee to whom he had been assigned, but he sat down and got involved right away, and with his own interest parried the second grader's attempts to push him away.

> I asked him if he had any homework and what he wanted to work on. He said he had math but it was easy and he could do it by himself in five minutes. I told him, "Show me, it's no rush,

I know you could probably do it in five minutes, but I want to do it along with you."

He acted as if he did not need me for the first thirty minutes. He was trying to prove how smart he was. When he got stuck on a problem, instead of asking me for help he would tell me how good he was in math and how he could do it so fast, trying to get off the subject. When I was showing him how to do it, he would snap and say, "I was getting to that." I told him that I was just trying to remember myself and was just discussing the problem myself.

Although this was no idyllic start for a tutoring session and the tutor was received with little enthusiasm, he stayed involved. Within twenty minutes, the tutee started to sprinkle the session with personal comments, letting the tutor into his life. The tutor could then demonstrate his desire for a sincere tutor-tutee relationship. By the end of the session, the math homework had become a game designed to *prevent* the child from making small talk.

Toward the end, he had problems sticking to the assignment, so I made a deal with him. If he could do one row of problems correctly in five minutes, I would buy him a candy bar of his choice. Although I encouraged our getting-acquainted conversations, I needed to have him complete the assignment also. I knew he could do it, but up to this point it was taking him five minutes to complete one problem.

He said, "Wait until the next line." I was fooled. He picked the line with two-digit problems as opposed to three-digit ones on the previous lines. I told him he was so smart, how he fooled me, now he could show me how well he knew his math. He was excited when I discovered he fooled me; he started cheering and almost ran out of time . . . we were really comfortable with

each other at this point, joking and teasing. I knew I had succeeded in gaining Javier's trust.

This tutor's enthusiasm for his work and interest in the child allowed a connection to be made. Javier's ability to fool the tutor and
to show what he knows and can do, and the tutor's acceptance of
his way of expressing himself, allowed the boy to feel more trust. It
also indicates the success you as a tutor can achieve through passion for your work and interest in your tutee.

FEELING EMPATHY

One of the biggest fears that many tutors face, and one that can be
the most crippling, is expressed in the question, *Will I like my tutee?*
It's hard to imagine working with a person you don't like or don't
approve of. But it's important to remember that liking your student
is not the most important aspect of the tutoring relationship. Your
student may not be the person you would choose as your best friend,
or a child you would want to adopt. Your tutee may be involved in
things, or do things, that you consider wrong or reprehensible.
None of this matters. Liking your tutee is not essential. Feeling empathy for your tutee is.

Empathy differs significantly from sympathy. We can empathize with someone whether or not we like their actions, because we can *understand* why the acts were committed. For
instance, when a student cheats on an exam, we may empathize
but not necessarily sympathize. We do not have to approve of
cheating. We do have to try to understand *why* the student
cheated. Was it too frightening to take the exam? Was the student
unable to study because of a lack of help or because a factor in the
home environment was too distracting the night before? If you
can understand what was behind the cheating, you can work with
the student and talk about it, while still maintaining the relationship.

In this example, a Latino tutor catches his ten-year-old tutee, Geraldo, cheating and works hard to understand the situation from the child's point of view.

I saw Geraldo as he was copying the answers from his neighbor, looking through the corner of his eye. I didn't want to make it obvious to the teacher, but I also wanted him to stop cheating. So I stared at him every chance I got. When our eyes met, almost at the end of the period, I could see the embarrassment on his face.

When the bell rang, he collected his stuff very quickly, to avoid talking to me, but I managed to catch him before he left. I did not need to say that I was disappointed in him, because his behavior indicated the acknowledgment of my disapproval and disappointment. But I told him that I understood why he was cheating and told him about an incident I had in my elementary years. Together we explored some other ways around the exam-induced anxiety he was facing, as well as his lack of preparation.

This tutor's empathy allowed him to explore and understand his tutee's situation without excusing the wrongful act. The result: new and effective lines of communication between the tutee and the tutor, through which they can arrive at a deeper understanding.

Once students discern that their tutor understands them and their situations from their perspectives, they in turn will be more eager to work with the tutor and more open to advice and suggestions. Certainly being a good listener signals to tutees that they are being understood. Empathy—understanding the tutee's position— is therefore fundamental to the development of a strong tutoring relationship.

One way to develop empathy is to believe that your tutees are doing the best they can. With this mindset, you will be less critical.

It's hard to criticize or condemn someone who cheats because they are afraid of failing and being beaten, ridiculed, or left behind a grade.

Even in situations where you patently disapprove of a student's values or actions, you can still empathize and still try to see where they are coming from. Only then can you respond to them in a way that makes sense to them and develop some kind of connection. In the following example, the tutor was working with the probation department, tutoring male juveniles who had just gotten out of lock-up. Although as an upper-middle-class white female graduate student she was continually surprised to learn of her students' crimes, which ranged from robbery to murder, this interaction really dumbfounded her.

> We were reading an article on police brutality and I asked the guys if they had been abused when they were arrested or while they were in lock-up. They said that of course they had, but that it hadn't been as severe as what we were reading about. We went on to have a really stimulating conversation about when brutality might be justified and when it wasn't. Byron and Trang were arguing over whether murderers have rights. Trang says that they don't, that they forfeit them when they kill someone. Byron isn't so sure.
>
> Later I asked Byron if he thought that all cops were bad. He said yes. Then he changed his mind. He said that not all of them were, but that he thought that the longer they had been on the street the worse they got. I asked why he thought that was. He said, "Well, they scared. They see so much. They tired of seeing it all." We talked about peer pressure from other police and if he thought that he could be a street cop. He struck me as so intelligent. He read really well and was really interested in talking.
>
> I asked him what he had been in for, he seemed so friendly and actually kind of sweet, I figured it would be minor.

"Burglarizing a house," he told me.

"Did you do it?"

"Yeah, I did it. But I would've gotten away with it if someone hadn't snitched on me. I'd have gotten away with it." I was kind of shocked. No remorse. Then he added, "But that just gonna slow me down."

I was really shocked, "What?"

"It just gonna slow me down." I could tell by his voice that he planned on keeping right on at it when he was done with his house arrest.

I kept flashing back to my friends who had just had their house robbed twice in one week, and who had lost a lot of valuables that they couldn't afford to replace. What could I say to this kid? Somehow I knew he wouldn't care about that. He won't sympathize with my friend whose laptop computer had gotten ripped off. He's never owned anything that valuable in his life. But I had to say something, "There are more honest ways to make money Byron. And the scariest thing about robbing houses isn't getting caught, it's the fact that the owner might have a gun, and he'll blow you away. No problem."

"Yeah, I guess you're right," he conceded.

It's hard to know if this tutor's reaction was the best one, if what she said would dissuade the student from committing his crime again. Perhaps she should have been stronger or more insistent. The point is that she could not and did not walk away, indignant. She did not lecture or moralize. She tried to think about the crime from his point of view and to suggest that something bad could happen to him. We don't know if the tutee understood, but she expressed her concern for the consequences of his actions in a way that showed her concern for him, not for her values and beliefs, which left room for further discussion—on this or other subjects the tutee might have hesitated to bring up.

This tutor will continue to teach Byron, even though she disapproves of his behavior. Rather than preaching to him, she will try as a role model and tutor to show him, rather than tell him, that there is a better way. This tutor did not need to like her student, but she needed to see where he was coming from and try to understand him. Then she could continue to interact with him and leave open the possibly of influencing him positively in the future.

Practices

These attitudes—giving up expectations, displaying enthusiasm and interest, and feeling empathy—lay the foundation for several successful general practices. These practices are *being patient, being observant and asking questions,* and *interacting with your student on as equal a level as possible*. For instance, being patient becomes a necessity once you give up your expectations. Because each tutoring partnership is unique, you must wait to learn about both your student and yourself. What sometimes seems to require an infinite amount of patience is worth it in the end. Being observant and asking questions are inherent in displaying interest and enthusiasm, the basic tools that show children that you are interested in and excited about working with them. Finally, you need to have empathy to understand students and work with them on an equal level. Each of these practices builds upon the other: being patient gives you the time to observe and ask relevant questions that bring you into the tutee's world.

PRACTICING PATIENCE

Patience can mean being willing to wait, or being understanding or tolerant, or enduring problems without complaint, or persevering in the face of adversity. In tutoring, patience means all these things. It's the ability (or the state of mind) to cope with discouraging situations and distracting environmental factors while focusing all your efforts on your tutee. It's being willing to let the student set the pace for the growth of the relationship and not being too pushy. It's being steadfast and trying one method after another until something clicks.

In the hospital case, the tutor showed patience by not allowing Brandon's refusal to talk discourage him. The tutor took his time and eventually came up with an effective way of interacting with Brandon, through his observation of environmental cues. Furthermore, he did not take the situation personally, realizing that there were many possible reasons for Brandon's behavior.

In the same way, you do not know what is going on in your tutee's life, and you should not assume anything. Children are more sincere and naturally more expressive than adults. They lack adults' enhanced ability to mask their problems and pretend that nothing is wrong. Remember, as discouraging as the situation may seem, your patience will allow your tutees to enjoy your company and see your sincere interest in them.

As the hospital volunteer reflected: "Although Brandon seemed not to care much about my presence, his actions talked a different language as he sacrificed two of his monkeys to guide me in the game. He also played Dynamite with me, which was indicative of a connection or a bond." The volunteer was patient, not presumptuous, and tried to approach Brandon from the boy's perspective by assessing the situation and observing important details.

Sometimes getting to know a student requires gentle probing, especially if you're thrown into a situation in which you know nothing about the tutee. Gentle probing is not always as easy as it sounds, and that is why patience is a necessary element. A student who is unhappy about being tutored or apathetic about schoolwork in general can shut down a shy tutor with relative ease. You will not always get, nor should you expect, immediate results. Sometimes an entire session or two may feel awkward, but every bit of information that you gather is a potential window into the student's life; store it all away, for it will eventually prove useful.

In the following case, a female tutor felt somewhat lost when her tutee arrived with no homework to work on and gave only terse answers to her questions. But in persevering, the tutor made some small connections, learned a little about her tutee, and was more prepared to get through to this student the next week.

My next student was nine-year-old Kim. There was no formal introduction except for names, so I fished for information. I asked, "Do you like school?"

Kim replied, "Some parts."

I went on, "What is your favorite subject?"

Her reply, "Math."

Kim's answers made it really difficult to perpetuate a conversation, but I forged on. "Do you like art?"

"No."

"Do you play sports?"

"No."

"Do you like music?"

"Oh yeah, I like music."

Finally something I could talk about. I mentioned to her that music and math are more alike than she probably thinks. For a moment she looked amused but then took on the boredom face again. I asked her, "Do you like any particular instrument?"

"No."

I thought, somewhere, she's got to give. "Okay, so who do you listen to?"

"I like Mariah Carey."

This tutor was not very familiar with Mariah Carey, so the student's comment did not lead to a serious connection. But the two kept talking, and the tutor finally found out that Kim had a boyfriend that she liked to talk about, and that she liked to go to the mall and would talk a little about those trips. Through a lot of effort on the tutor's part, the sessions eventually became more comfortable. The tutor only needed to gather up enough parts of her student's life to try to understand her and make her feel comfortable. Exercising patience and observing details about your tutees may likewise help you forge a connection.

BEING OBSERVANT AND ASKING QUESTIONS

Having given up expectations and developed the practice of patience, a tutor is in the best possible mindset for making observations. You can learn a lot about your tutees by noticing their body language, clothing, stickers on their binders, or the cassette in their Walkman. By being observant, you can pick up many details about tutees that can help you connect with them. In the hospital case, for example, the tutor's observation of the dinosaurs on Brandon's shelf—external cues in his environment—led him to plan an effective activity. Being observant is not limited to what you can see, however; it includes what you can learn through interaction. For instance, in Kim's case, the tutor learned of Kim's interest in music through their conversation.

Being observant takes effort, practice, and concentration. Yet it pays off, for every cue serves as a brick in building a successful tutoring experience. Observation helps in first-day situations especially, when it can alleviate much of the tension and awkwardness associated with first-day interaction. These crucial initial stages lead to a more effective learning environment, especially when tutees feel that you are involved in their lives. The cues you gather will enhance your understanding of your student, so that you can fine-tune an individual, appropriate approach for each tutee.

INTERACTING AS AN EQUAL

Interacting with your tutees as an equal requires pulling all the attitudes and practices we have talked about under one umbrella. It means patiently observing your tutees and trying to understand what motivates and excites them. It means accepting them unconditionally and giving up all your expectations of how they should be or how your interaction should proceed. Although this equal interaction is not easy to achieve, it marks the beginning of the success of your tutoring relationship. It proves to your students that you are really interested in them, not in disciplining, harassing, or changing them.

Tutoring is not an easy experience; as a tutoring relationship progresses, tutors are forced to face their own shortcomings and insecurities. But they also learn to work through them. In other words, tutor and tutee learn and grow together. As one tutor reflected, "It is the best feeling in the world. I am a part of him, and he is a part of me."

Recommended Reading

A number of excellent books describe teachers' efforts to work one-on-one or with small groups of students. Tutors, especially, will find the experiences of these gifted tutors and teachers rewarding and inspiring. In *36 Children* (1967), Herbert Kohl, a white, male teacher, succeeds in an all-black classroom in Harlem. In *Teacher* (1963), Sylvia Ashton-Warner, a white, British teacher, finds effective ways to teach Maori children in New Zealand. A Brazilian educator, Paulo Freire, develops an active model for teaching adults in *Pedagogy of the Oppressed* (1989). For a model of how Japanese teachers approach and impact children, read *Educating Hearts and Minds* (1995) by Catherine Lewis.

Wonderful books on children's thinking are *How Children Learn* (1983) and *How Children Fail* (1982) by John Caldwell Holt. Numerous studies show that children benefit from spending time with adults and talking and reading with them. For more on this and how various interactions with adults affect children's school achievement, see Catherine Snow's "Literacy and Language: Relationships during the Preschool Years" (1983).

2
Building Relationships

One of the most vital steps in the development of the tutor-tutee relationship concerns exactly that, creating a relationship. Superficially, tutoring looks easy, particularly if the students are young and the material simple. But tutors are on hand to provide not only answers to students but moral and emotional support and to ferret out exactly what areas the student needs help in. What would be an extremely difficult process between strangers occurs naturally between two people who have come to know and care about each other.

Creating a strong personal relationship with your tutee is vital. Without it, a tutor can, at best, scratch the surface of a student's needs. To help a child with an assignment may improve a homework grade or even raise the score on an upcoming test, but to fill in long-standing gaps in knowledge or to help a child grasp more complex concepts, the tutor needs to understand what the student does not know and must devise ways to introduce this information to the student. The best tutor will find ways to use children's natural curiosity and interest to motivate them to *want* to master challenges and learn.

Although some tutoring relationships are long and enduring, many are relatively brief encounters: a semester, a few weeks or months. The biggest impact that tutors can make is not in higher test scores or better spelling papers, but in the learning techniques and confidence that one-on-one work can instill in a child. Built on a personal connection, the tutoring experience can leave a lifelong impression on both tutor and child. But making this connection and achieving this level of intimacy requires forging a strong relationship with the student.

Not that all tutor-tutee relationships are equally easy to build. Myriad potential barriers usually stand between any particular tutoring pair and a strong tutoring relationship. Many tutors work with children of a different gender, race, age, or socioeconomic background than their own. Many find themselves dealing with a tutee with emotional and family problems that the tutors do not feel fully equipped to handle. Other tutors find that they struggle with the educational system, either in conflicts with teachers or in dealing with a tutee who has been labeled somehow inferior and whose self-esteem suffers as a result. (We explore these potential problems, and the ways many tutors have chosen to handle them, in later chapters.) The authors' experience suggests that most of these barriers can be overcome; to create a successful tutoring situation, they *must* be overcome.

Few barriers are insurmountable, although some may be daunting. How do you deal with an unmotivated student? Or a student who won't talk to you? Breaking down the walls often begins with *making some small connection*. Find a way to close the gap between you and the child, even if it has nothing to do with academics. Getting students to talk about their soccer team or a favorite movie is sometimes enough to open them up a little, and to let them see you as a person.

From this tiny crack, tutors can continue to open the door by *building rapport and trust with their students*, a complex process. Tutors must be willing to listen and be there for their students. They may also need to give something of themselves in order to show some reciprocity in the relationship. Another of the most important steps in tutoring, this process begins to move the relationship from dependence toward autonomy. Although the ultimate goal of a tutoring or mentoring relationship is to empower the students with independent skills and a love for learning, the only way to instill them is through a trust-based relationship. The tutees must come to depend on you, the tutor, as a stable and constant influence they can rely on. With this trust and dependence in place, you can pass on the strength that will make your tutees independent when tutoring ends.

Once some degree of trust has been established, the tutor has laid the foundation for a relationship and builds on it to *motivate the student to learn*. Although tutors should try to enter the tutoring site without the burden of expectations, by the time they have established relationships with children, it is not only acceptable but desirable to formulate *educated expectations* of what tutees can accomplish. Tutors can use these new grounded expectations as leverage with the students to motivate them to learn.

The motivation that a tutor can encourage in a child extends *beyond academics*. Tutors are role models and adult figures in the lives of their tutees. Young people frequently seek to understand the world of adults and hope to emulate the adults they admire. In many cases some things you own or have attained that perhaps may not mean a lot to you are things your tutees aspire to have or do— among them, going to a university, holding a "cool" job, excelling in sports or music, having your own apartment or car, having a boyfriend or girlfriend, or traveling. Building upon the relationship of tutor and tutee, the tutor can encourage and motivate a student to pursue possibilities and ambitions well beyond the completion of homework assignments.

As with any relationship, the participants in a good tutor-tutee partnership work on the *establishment of boundaries to create a balanced relationship*. Boundaries are essential to maintain a working relationship, and the tutor and tutee must negotiate them together in order to set limits that both are comfortable with. Although making the tutee feel at home is one of the essentials of tutoring, an uncomfortable *tutor* is a less effective tutor. Setting boundaries that preserve the camaraderie of the relationship while maintaining the tutor's authority can prove a delicate balancing act, constantly negotiated throughout the relationship.

Like other relationships, each tutoring combination offers a unique experience, but, having followed the experiences of hundreds of tutors, we have a great deal of confidence in tutors' ability to bond with their students and not only help them to improve their schoolwork but to shape and inform their lives.

Making Connections

The first thing that a tutor must do with a new tutee is make some kind of connection. How tutors make connections differs according to the personal interaction styles of both student and tutor. But, as with any relationship, some common ground must be established to create the space for the tutoring relationship to grow. Sometimes these connections are purely academic; a child needs help with math or some kind of homework assignment, and the tutor is there to provide it. Other times connections are more personal—a favorite food, sports team, or music group, or an ethnic background that the tutor and tutee share. To establish a connection, a tutor must be a careful observer, particularly at the outset of tutoring. An astute tutor can usually find some way to achieve that magical moment in an early session when things seem to click with a student. It is, of course, important to remember that these connections are not always made without a great deal of effort.

Responding to a Request for Help

A tutee's request for help is often the first step in building a relationship with a tutee, especially with an older or adult student. But neither the relationship nor the academic help stops once the question has been answered. Talk to your students; if they don't understand a concept, move back a step—there's a good chance they don't understand the preceding concepts either. Students, especially when they first meet a tutor, are reluctant to ask for clarification. They may tell you that they understand even when they are still confused. Encourage them to keep talking, to explain processes back to you. Make it clear that you will explain as many times and in as many different ways as it takes to help them understand.

Many tutors find this helping process an ice breaker. Even if the student does not open up immediately, it opens the door for future contact, making it easier for the student to interact with the tutor in later sessions. Sometimes a student who leaves the first tutoring session still shy and reserved asks for help right away the next week. Tutees may wait to see if you appear again before they begin to trust you. Just showing up again can prove that you are there for them.

Picking up on an Interest

Tutors often find it much easier to get close to younger students than to older ones. Many try to make an immediate connection, to get the children smiling and ready to let down their walls a little. Comment on a baseball cap with a team name on it, or a T-shirt with a Disney character. Show the children that you're interested in who they are and what they like. In the process you demonstrate a great deal: that the tutoring sessions don't follow the same rigid structure as school, that you are interested in more than just the children's academic progress, and that they can relax and be themselves with you.

This tutor found that commonalties established something of a connection but that she needed to work a little harder to build a strong bond with her tutee, a fourteen-year-old, ninth-grade Latino student.

Marco reminded me of Robert from *36 Children* because among his books was a sketch pad containing some amazing works of art. One in particular, an intricate drawing of a joker, contained the words, "Breathe in, breathe out." It comes from a song by the band Bush, so I immediately asked Marco if he listened to that type of music (alternative) and he said yes. We smiled at each other approvingly, making our first connection. At first he did not look me in the eyes either, but as soon as I asked him about his work everything changed.

"What is that?" I asked, referring to a leather-bound black notebook.

"Oh, I draw sometimes, you know."

"Can I see one?" I dared, hoping I wouldn't be rejected.

"If you want." I breathed a sigh of relief as he handed the book over.

"It's a joker," he said pointing to it.

"That's really good, Marco!" I said with sincerity.

His eyes met mine for the first time. He even smiled, "Thanks."

One tutor who was having a particularly hard time getting through to a shy ten-year-old girl in the fifth/sixth-grade class she was working with had a breakthrough when she complimented the child.

I complimented Brianne on her white shoes she was wearing and told her how I liked how her name was painted in different colors on the outside. I asked her who made those for her, and she replied her aunt. She then began to say how her aunt does her hair and braids it for her. I told her that her hair was so beautiful and long. She told me she would braid mine like hers if I wanted her to. I said, "OK," not thinking she wanted to braid right there and then.

> Brianne was very talented, and she braided my hair in two minutes. I praised her over and over again on how good my braid looked. She then said, smiling, "We look like sisters and twins, too."

The utterance "We look like sisters and twins, too" demonstrates the strong sense of identification that children have, often over things that adults are likely to dismiss as silly or simple. Remember that making a connection can be much easier than it looks at a first glance.

If nothing triggers a connection immediately, talk to your students. See what they like and dislike. Ask them what they do for fun and who their friends are and what they like to do outside school. Take mental notes. Remembering a topic from one session to the next can serve as proof that you care and are truly interested. Even if a child is not willing to discuss something immediately, you may be able to bring it up or work it into an activity later and make a connection.

Other times, as you work toward making a connection, something will fall into place. Because these two female tutors not only persisted but remained relaxed with their first-grade African American student, they found a commonality with her that they never could have imagined.

> After school I tutored a first-grade African American girl named Tumaini. She was very quiet at first. She sat down and kept her head down even when she talked. When I began talking to her, she answered almost in a whisper, with her face down and her hands in her face.
>
> She was the only tutee to come after school so Sara and I decided to tutor her together. We introduced ourselves and then asked her questions, such as, what is her favorite color and how many siblings did she have. She answered, "Pink, and my

sister who goes to another school and takes the bus will pick me up at 3:30 P.M."

When we asked her, "Do you have homework?," she brought out two handouts. One was a picture of a flower with four blank squares at the bottom. The assignment was to draw the steps showing how the flower grew. We began by asking her what was needed first to make a flower, and she said, "Seeds." She then drew them and continued by drawing a person planting them and watering them. During this assignment she was still very quiet. She did answer our questions, but only in a whisper with her head down and her hands in her face.

Her second assignment was to write the months on a long gray paper with wide lines. As soon as we saw the paper, Sara and I began reminiscing about our school days when we used that paper. We told Tumaini that the paper always tore when you erased. She laughed and said that that happened to her too. It was this discussion that helped her feel comfortable with us because she began to speak louder. She removed her hands from her face when she spoke to us and she made eye contact.

As in this example, patience usually leads to a breakthrough or a connection. Sometimes this "getting to know you" period can also act as a gateway to a more enjoyable school activity that the student would be reluctant to do otherwise. In the next exchange, a male Filipino tutor remembered an interest of his nine-year-old Latino student and used it to get him interested in reading in the extra time that they had together: "I thought maybe we could read a book like *Goosebumps* or something like that. He had mentioned reading one of R. L. Stine's *Goosebumps* books before in a previous session. I recalled the story he was explaining to me called *Be Careful What You Wish For* and got him talking about it again. Like many of the other stories he had told me up to that point, he was really excited and tended to stutter over words."

Later, drawing on his student's interest in myths and science fiction, the same tutor brought in Filipino fables and myths, both to make for some interesting reading and to share some of his culture with his tutee.

In some situations, creating a connection proves difficult, and the tutor will have to exert more effort, sometimes for fewer rewards. But even without speaking it is possible to create a link between yourself and a tutee. For instance, in the case of the hospitalized child discussed in Chapter 1, the tutor tried everything he could think of to get the boy to open up, to no avail. He finally took some visual cues from the child's personal effects and went to work trying to find some game or activity to break the child out of his shell. Although the experience ended without any words exchanged, the tutor left with some feeling of accomplishment. He had managed to show the child that he understood where his interests lay and that he respected the child's decision not to talk at that moment. Wordlessly, he had made a connection.

Avoiding Gifts and Bribes

One temporarily effective and common method of making a connection has a tendency to backfire: tutors sometimes find that the easiest way to win the friendship of a child is to bring candy or gifts to the tutoring session. This trap is easy to fall into. Even the most stubborn child will probably crack when presented with a candy bar or new stickers. The tutee will even look forward to the tutor's return.

For the most part, this is a technique to avoid. Bringing gifts creates a superficial bond between tutor and child, and returning the following week without candy or gifts will invariably endanger the relationship. Gifts or rewards presented regularly can undermine the tutoring because the tutee begins to focus on the goodies rather than learning. Constant gifts can also hurt the relationship;

they tend to preclude a deeper partnership built on trust and common interests.

The following example shows how fragile a relationship built on bribes can be. This tutor found that she had no emotional or personal leverage with the ten-year-old African American girl she had been working with. Her requests meant nothing, only the candy her tutee, Summer, had come to expect.

> I said, "Summer, come here and sit down. Mr. Brick wants you to read this short story and answer the questions on the back. We only have twenty minutes left so you better start reading it."
>
> Summer placed her hands on her hips and stated, "I don't want to read that stupid story."
>
> While she walked away, I replied, "Fine, then, I won't give you the candy I brought you."
>
> "You better give it to me!"
>
> "Nope, not until you read."
>
> With an angry look, Summer left and went to sit at her desk.

Although a child will usually respond to bribes, the loyalty that results is often short-lived.

Building Trust

Making a connection is key to establishing a good tutoring relationship, but it is only one small step. From that step the whole process of creating a relationship begins. One of the main foundations of this relationship must be trust, which a tutor can build in many ways. Sometimes it is just a matter of proving that you, as the tutor, are there to help and that you care. Other times tutees demand some kind of reciprocity before they will open up to you. In still other cases, the tutor must prove, by remembering facts about a tutee's life and showing genuine interest, that the tutee is an important part of the tutor's life.

As you go about the process of building trust, you are not only trying to get your tutee to depend on you, but you want to be worthy of the dependence. Of course you will make a conscientious effort not to disappoint your student (as in arriving late or not at all), but you also have the obligation to make sure that the new ideas you pass on contribute to the ultimate goal of tutoring: a student with an increased sense of strength, independence, and love for learning.

Overcoming Past Experiences

Trust is the most precarious aspect of a tutoring relationship to establish. Although some students give it easily, many are suspicious. Establishing trust can be especially hard when students in tutoring programs have seen several tutors come and go, some without saying good-bye. Other students have experienced apathetic tutors and don't know how to even go about establishing a real relationship with a tutor. The following is a conversation that one tutor had with a staff member as she was introduced to her site, a private school for emotional disturbed adolescents.

> As Torey continued to tell me about the school, there must have been some sort of excitement in my eyes because Torey asked if I was nervous. I said no, but that I was excited to begin working with the school. I asked why he thought I was nervous. He indicated that previous tutors were never this excited to work with the students. I said, "What do you mean?" He said that a lot of tutors signed in and went to their corner to read their books or magazines.

The same tutor experienced a rude awakening on her first day of tutoring at this school.

Ms. Smith's [the teacher] students seemed well behaved: they quietly attended to their work. While I mentioned this to Ms. Smith, she laughed and said, "You haven't seen nothing yet." I continued monitoring the surroundings. A young lady raised her hand, her eyes directed toward me. Ms. Smith asked her what she needed. The young lady asked Ms. Smith who I was. Ms. Smith told her that I was from UCLA and that I would be helping her out in the classroom. I said hello. She said hi and asked me what my major was. I responded, "Sociology and psychology." She responded with, "Oh, I get it, another lab experiment."

Tutees will often express their opinions directly and without embarrassment. And this student's reaction to her new tutor demonstrates that every tutor who works with a student leaves a legacy. When students have a bad experience with a tutor, they remember. This memory can affect their progress not only with that tutor, but with every tutor they come in contact with. That's why, as you move through your tutoring experience, it is important to bear in mind that you are creating a long-lasting impact on your tutee.

Tutors can just as easily leave a good as a bad tutoring legacy, a tutee who remains eager to work with other mentors. Many students remember good experiences with tutors, and their memories show that these relationships are often important ones to them. A Latino sixth grader who opened up fairly easily to his new tutor "shared with me that his old tutor had gone to Switzerland and that he had sent him a postcard. He seemed really touched by that."

It's important to keep trying and to remain available. Some of the best ways to gain the respect and trust of your tutees (even leery ones) are to be straightforward and honest with them, to respect their individuality, and to lay out the parameters, or the possible parameters, of the relationship from the start.

Showing Respect

Tutors can build trust, which lays the foundation for the tutoring experience, in numerous ways. First, tutors need to generate an atmosphere of mutual respect. They serve as role models for tutees, so it's important for the tutor to be someone whom the tutee can look up to and admire. The tutees' respect for their tutors also plays an important role in how well they listen to and follow their suggestions regarding academic work.

It is just as vital for tutors to respect their tutees. Student capabilities vary widely, but it is not for the tutor to judge whether students are up to par. The tutor is there to help and encourage the students while still giving them the respect and autonomy that every person, including children, deserves.

One of the hardest things for tutors to understand is how difficult it is for many students to ask for help. Often their reluctance stems from pride, and the same inhibition that prevents students from raising a hand in class to ask a question can cause them to be shy with a tutor. Why should children make themselves vulnerable to a stranger? Tutors must be patient, not push too hard, but make sure that students know that they are open to and available for questions. Tutees should know that their tutors won't think any less of them for asking for help, that in fact tutors welcome their questions.

One tutor working at a community center geared toward teaching leadership to mostly minority high school students found that she had to be very tactful about offering her help so that she didn't offend the students she was working with.

The black male, whose name is Jesse, said that he was doing fine and that he did not need a tutor. "Tutors make you feel stupid," said Jesse. I looked quickly at him and asked him what he meant by that. He just said that some tutors can make you feel stupid by the way they talk to you. I asked him if I had made him feel stupid by asking him if he needed help. "Nah," he said.

"Okay, well, if you need help, then I'll help you; if not, that's okay too," I told him. He smiled and then went about his work. I just sat there and laughed—hoping to ease the tension.

It was a rocky start, but because this tutor backed off and respected the pride involved in this young man's asking for help, he was able, after a few minutes, to get assistance from her, and they went on to form a close relationship. The next week, Jesse asked for help as soon as his tutor walked in.

The basis of this relationship was actually created by this tutor's willingness to *let the student determine his own needs*. This is a major part of the relationship. Unlike teachers who have to manage a classroom full of students, tutors get to individualize their attention. This means that they can negotiate teaching styles and subjects with their students, giving the students a sense of autonomy and making the academic help much more valuable.

Another tricky area that many tutors run into is a tendency, perhaps because of their own discomfort or unease, to treat their students like toddlers—the opposite of giving students respect and autonomy and allowing them to determine their own needs. Sometimes tutors resort to using baby talk with their students, or they hover over students, giving the impression that they consider them incapable of working on their own. Such behavior not only strips students of their independence, it demeans them and deprives them of the notion that they even deserve respect.

Although tutors often enter the tutoring site expecting to sit right down and work with a student, it may take the student awhile to get used to the presence of another "teacher." Tutors should not appear standoffish, but by giving students the space they need, tutors can help establish themselves as people the students will want to form relationships with.

Tutors can also actively foster mutual respect in their relationship with their tutees by showing that they value them—their feelings and their friendship. The following white female tutor was able to show respect for Estella, her seven-year-old Latina tutee, in two ways: by respecting the possibility that Estella might be jealous of her tutor's other tutee and by asking for a piece of her artwork.

> The time went by very quickly, and before I knew it, it was 5:00 and almost time for Jake to arrive. I politely told Estella that we had to finish up because it was almost time for her to go home and my next kid to come. She did not know that I tutored someone else. The last thing I wanted was for her to think that I was trying to get rid of her.
>
> "You tutor someone else?" she asked.
>
> "Yeah, after you go home, a boy named Jake comes and I help him out with his homework and talk like we do. But you know what? He doesn't like to draw beautiful rainbows like you do."
>
> She smiled and then asked, "Can I take that picture [that her tutor had drawn] home?"
>
> "If you get to take one of mine, then I get to take one of yours." I asked her what pictures I could keep, and we exchanged pictures and she went inside to pack up.

In allowing her tutee to keep her drawing, the tutor gave Estella something of herself to hold onto until the next week. By the same token, by asking for Estella's drawing, the tutor demonstrated that she valued her time with Estella and wanted to keep part of that interaction with her.

Establishing Reciprocity

Another way a tutor can create trust in the tutoring relationship is by sharing personal stories and experiences with students. As a tutor, you are in a position of authority. But as the personal helper of a student, you stand to be much more than just a smaller-scale teacher. Good tutors can hope to have students open up to them and expose their passions and interests. These insights form the basis for a relationship, and they are also what makes individual tutoring such a rewarding experience. But before students open up, they often need to see that sharing is a two-way street, that the tutor is not just another authority figure there to exploit them or to make them vulnerable.

Sharing personal information can be a delicate part of the tutoring relationship; students like to get personal. And when you have a successful tutoring relationship, in which you are a mentor as well as a role model and friend, this is natural. Some students are just curious. Others may be testing you to see if you are who you say you are and if you are willing to play an equal role in the relationship. It's a fine line for a tutor to walk. How much do you want to tell this child? Many tutors find it useful to share personal information. Often, the sharing creates a more personal connection with the students, particularly if you find that you have something important in common or if you have some expertise in an area they are interested in.

Many tutors find that students respond well to the sharing of personal anecdotes by their tutor. This tutor, for example, drew on resources from her personal experience to advise her tutee, a student at an alternative high school.

> We talked about where he wanted to go and he said he is first going to a local community college, then wants to transfer to

UCLA. I told him that's the best way to save money and get all your G.E.s [general education requirements] done before transferring, but I told him not to be one that gets caught in the community college forever. I told him that it is easy to slack off because no one is there to motivate you but you. I told him that I went to community college and then transferred to UCLA as a junior. I told him that he should follow the IGETC [a form that tells junior college students what classes are transferable and count toward a major at a four-year university].

We figured out that he will be able to transfer after a year and a half if he continues to take the right amount of units. He got excited and I recommended that he even take summer school to lessen his load during the year; he started laughing because I was so into it. I think that Bob was willing to hear my advice because I think he realized that I went through the system and was able to transfer.

Other times a tutor can offer personal information as a reward or a validation that the friendship is in fact a two-way street. Sometimes little intimacies that prove a true relationship exists can be the most rewarding parts of tutoring. In the following episode, Juliette, the tutor whose tutee, Jesse, told her that some tutors can make you feel stupid, establishes a bond in that way.

When I approached his table, he [Jesse] moved over so I could sit next to him. He continued to work on his algebra problem but stopped halfway when he realized he didn't know what to do. "Hey, Jul, can you help me here?"

"Sure, what's the problem, Jes?" I responded with a laugh.

He looked at me strangely and said, "Huh?"

"Well, you did call me 'Jul,' so I figured I could call you 'Jes,'" I said to him. He responded with a smile.

Here is a six-year-old tutee being a gentleman and a friend: "Soon we went back inside the center because it was getting dark and cold. Jose had taken off his large sweatshirt earlier and offered to let me wear it because I was cold. It covered my arms and for that I was grateful." Jose's offering of the sweatshirt and his tutor's gracious acceptance, although not a practice customary in a teaching relationship, reflects the types of mutual respect and personal regard that tutors and tutees can create.

There will be times, however, when students' questions cross a line, and tutors may feel uncomfortable answering. It is up to tutors to draw the line wherever they feel comfortable. Some kids will push their tutor as far as they can, as did this eleven-year-old male student.

> Juan asked me a lot of personal questions, although not all at once or right off the bat. One of the first questions he asked was if I lived with a roommate. I answered that I lived with my boyfriend and found myself feeling a little embarrassed. He didn't ask anything further about that; he went back to his work. He asked if I was "a volunteer or doing tutoring through school." I told him through school, and he asked, "How old are you?" And when I told him thirty, he said, "Shouldn't you be done with school?" I explained that I decided to go back to college because I hadn't finished my degree.

Putting the child at ease by sharing personal information does little good if you feel uncomfortable as a result. In the case of Juan and his tutor, even though the tutor did not feel completely comfortable sharing all this information, the exchange formed the basis of what became a close tutoring relationship.

Not every situation is easy. A tutor, a Persian male, was enjoying his interaction with his eight-year-old Persian tutee because of their similar ethnic backgrounds and her natural curiosity about college life. In the course of the conversation, Mary said that her mother would punish her if she mentions even the mildest bad word. The tutor, feeling confident about being able to further their camaraderie, offered the following story:

> "My father never physically beat me except once in my entire life."
>
> "What did you do?" Mary asked.
>
> "I called him a very bad name."
>
> "What did you call him?"
>
> Soon I realized the hole I had dug for myself. Had I not told her, she would be disappointed in me and not share anything with me. Had I told her, I would run the risk of teaching her a bad word. This created a serious dilemma, so I explained to her why I couldn't tell her the word, but she insisted and threatened to not tell me anything. So my only way out was to choose one of the words that she was throwing out there (which she obviously already knew), in guessing what I called my father.

In this case, the release of too much information created an awkward situation for the tutor that could be alleviated only with a white lie. In sharing personal information, discretion and sometimes careful maneuvering will be involved. In the end, tutors have to make their own choices about how much to share—but tutors who expect children to open up to them will probably have to trust them with some of their own personal experiences.

How quickly kids open up to their tutors varies considerably, sometimes along age and gender lines, sometimes according to students' personalities. These fifth-grade girls were eager to let their new female tutor into their circle: "When I was leaving, the four girls from my group ran up to me and gave me a hug and asked if I will be here tomorrow. I told them not 'til next week, and they said they can't wait. I was really excited when I was leaving because I felt like the children really enjoyed me being there and I felt a close friendship forming with them."

A Few Practical Concerns

With the myriad complex and personal issues that affect building and sustaining trust in a tutoring relationship, there are a few practical concerns to keep in mind. The building of trust is a long and careful process that can be destroyed easily. When you create a relationship, you ask your student to trust you, which carries with it some obligations on your part. Among them: (1) showing up for tutoring sessions, and showing up on time; (2) calling ahead and rescheduling if for some reason you must miss a session; (3) keeping your promises—if you promise to bring something to a session, such as a book or some information, do it.

The following tutor found that her failure to follow up compromised some of the progress she had made in their previous session with her tutee, a fourteen-year-old Latina:

Laura was more pleasant with me this second time around, touching me on the arm when she arrived. As I was already on the computer, she went ahead and sat down with me. She said she wanted to compose something again. I was a flake. I had promised Laura that I would type up the letter about her late friend Joaquin, but had not delivered on that promise. I told her that I would get it to her definitely by next week. She just kind of smiled and nodded, not upset and not necessarily disbelieving. I don't know, I couldn't read her reaction. I was so upset with myself though, that I had already broken that promise.

As intuitive and personal as tutoring relationships are, sometimes it's the concrete stuff that proves their solidity. Keeping promises means a lot to children. It proves that they can count on you.

Motivating Students to Learn

For a tutor, forming a relationship can sometimes feel like a waste of time. Shouldn't a tutor use every second to help with the child's schoolwork? Not necessarily. Often, time invested in getting to know a tutee can make the time spent learning even more valuable. Once relationships are formed, tutors can work within them to help their tutees overcome their academic problems.

A strong relationship with a child provides several opportunities. You can use your knowledge of a child to gear schoolwork toward particular interests and learning patterns. You can provide moral support just by being there as the child works. You can bargain with the student and use the relationship as leverage. And you can use your *educated expectations* of the student to set goals for learning. All these techniques contribute to the tutoring experience, because tutoring is much more than sharing academic knowledge. It's motivating kids to enjoy learning and to feel good about themselves while they do it. One woman who has been a tutor for almost ten years stated it this way: "*The* most important aspect of my job is to be a good cheerleader."

Applying Tutee Interests

Drawing children out and getting them interested in learning can prove one of the most difficult parts of tutoring. How do you orient children to tasks that they fear or are not interested in? One of the best ways to overcome this difficulty is to apply the task to something that they *are* interested in, or that they feel confident about. This tutor, a white female who aspires to be a special education teacher, finally got her fourth-grade African American student, Brad, to open up to her by indulging him and letting him tell stories. Terrified at the thought of reading or writing, Brad was an eager and competent storyteller and quickly lost his inhibitions when he got into a narrative mode.

Brad started to turn away from the table, but I wanted to get the tutoring session under control, so I immediately asked him if he would like to read one of the books on outer space. Brad, however, had something else in mind. "I would like to tell some stories."

Mr. Brick suggested that he wanted the students to direct their own session whenever possible. So, since today was our session, I thought it would be good to let Brad lead. I also was curious about this virus he had mentioned and so I thought that if I were to listen to his stories I might have a better idea of where Brad is coming from and where his interests lie. So I said, "Brad, why don't you tell me a story?" Brad responded by saying he had a really good story to tell me.

He walked away from the desk, stood about ten feet away from me, and then started to tell a story about UFOs that were coming down to Earth to fight the bad people. I faced my chair toward him and leaned forward so that he knew I was taking interest in what he was telling me. Brad began to pace back and forth on the carpet and showed no signs of nervousness as he told his UFO story. Sometimes Brad would look down at the floor and other times he would look up at the wall, and he would always look over at me to make sure I was listening. I couldn't even pick up on everything he was saying since he was talking so fast.

Brad would tell his story in third person, then he would have his characters talk in dialogue form. When Brad liked a certain part of the story that he was talking about, his eyes would get big and his voice would change to higher tones, even spit would start coming out of his mouth. Brad stopped pacing on the carpet and began walking around the room as he continued to tell his story. I got the impression that he was gathering ideas from the props, books, posters in the room to help him add to his story. I kept saying to myself, Is this the quiet, underconfident boy that I was helping last week in math? I couldn't get over Brad's imagination, which brought him to life and gave him confidence and an automatic smile across his face.

After about twenty minutes of storytelling, the tutor was beginning to feel guilty because she had been working with Brad all morning without getting him to do any reading or writing; she had been letting him tell her monster stories. She came up with the idea of having Brad tell his story into a tape recorder and then writing and illustrating his own book. Brad, who had said only a few words to his tutor before he got into storytelling mode, was thrilled the next week when she arrived with a tape recorder and book-making materials.

I told him that not only was he going to tell another story but that I would record him telling his story. At this point he was sitting down at the desk and a wide smile came across his face and his eyes got really big. Brad seemed very excited about the idea, and I asked him if he had ever heard his voice recorded. He said that he hadn't and gave a chuckle as he put his hands on top of his head.

Brad asked me why we had these school supplies with us—now I could explain to him that not only were we going to record his story, but that we were also going to make a book about his story. Once I told him the plan he couldn't stop talking about what we could do with the book after it was complete. He made some suggestions like, "Yeah, let's make it really good so I can sell it to people."

This project turned into one in which Brad drew his own illustrations, put together the book, and sounded out the words of his story to write it down. Brad was reading, writing, and drawing, and he was excited about it, something that never would have happened if Brad's tutor hadn't listened to his stories and found out what got him excited—what would make him eager to learn. Taking the time to form a relationship allowed this tutor to peer into the mind of her tutee and focus in on the best ways to motivate him into doing activities that intimidated him. This is another example of how respecting the wishes of tutees and giving them some autonomy in their learning process can open doors to a fruitful relationship.

Paying attention to what a tutee enjoys can also lead you to *how* the child likes to learn and what methods will be the most effective. This tutor was frustrated at the lack of motivation his seventh-grade African American student displayed and was trying to find a way to make fractions interesting. In some of their extra time, as he watched his student draw and teach some other students to draw, he gained insight into his tutee.

He reached once again down into his oversized pockets and pulled out a folded up piece of paper. He opened it and showed me a drawing that he made with a friend's instruction that morning in school. This was a really good drawing. I don't mean good as in nice attempt, I mean good in objective quality. So we talked about this art friend of his and how he was teaching Jonathon to draw all sorts of cool monsters, three-dimensional shapes, and fancy lettering of all kinds. It was something he talked fondly of and looked forward to every day in school—the fifteen minutes in homeroom when he was learning to draw. I asked him to draw me other things, and without much hesitation he proceeded to draw his name in creative bubble lettering. Then he drew a dog and some other animals.

It was clear that each figure he drew was not just a natural inclination he had to draw, but a routinized form taken on through learning. Let me explain: the puppy dog that he drew started with two round circles, and I was stumped as to which part of the dog they would end up being. Then with a few more strokes of his favorite three-dollar mechanical pencil, the animal started taking on recognizable shape. He had learned patterns and could incorporate them into different figures and characters. While at first I thought this was a diversion, it later appeared to me to be the very thing that weekly fractions were not, an activity by which Jonathon could be motivated to learn.

With this new information, the tutor knew that his tutee was not opposed to learning. He found out that Jonathon could be eager to learn, as long as he was interested in what was being taught.

Providing Companionship

Doing schoolwork with a "friend" sometimes makes the work more fun—even if it's just a math worksheet or something that would otherwise be boring and rote. As the tutor quoted earlier suggested, the most important part of her job as a tutor is being a cheerleader. She said that she knew that she could not make much of an academic difference with children in just a few weeks or months, but that improving their confidence and pumping up their self-image were of great importance. This approach has proved useful for many tutors: simply getting students excited about learning.

Julia was not very fond of math, especially for a lesson that asked you to subtract using the concept of borrowing.

"You and I, my friend, are going to work on subtraction! Just you and I, okay? Are you ready?" I asked.

"Yeah," she responded.

"Okay then, let's have a high five to get started." At which point she gave me a high five and smiled.

Other times tutors can provide important support and encouragement as they help their students with a concept they struggle with. Sometimes a little advice and some positive feedback is enough. The following white female tutor found that her fourth-grade Mexican American student tended to give up because she was afraid of what she didn't know. The tutor gave her not only a tip on how to get around those kinds of problems, but some confidence along with it.

Inside the gym, I sit in between two girls and have them work on independent problems. They both get to the same question about ears of corn, that I have to admit is a little tricky. I have to read the question several times over to understand what it is asking. (I wonder if the girls notice I'm struggling and tell them I think the problem is tough also.) I go through the problem step-by-step, learning as I go along. We get to a part that requires them to multiply twelve times eight. Jennifer turns to her own booklet and works away at the problem. I'm watching her carry the one, when I notice that Gina is not looking at her book.

"Do you need some help?"

Silence.

"Do you know how to multiply twelve times eight?"

Small tears roll down her cheeks as she looks at her lap and puts her hand to her face. I am totally confused. Did I do something? Did I not do something? What do I do? Jennifer is still working when I have Gina take a walk with me to the gym's stairs. I didn't want to ask her why she is upset in front of Jennifer. I don't think she will tell me the truth.

"I don't know my twelve times tables," she ekes out with a silent sob.

"Do you know how to multiply eight times two?"

"Yeah, sixteen."

"What is eight times one, plus one?" There was a long pause.

"Nine."

"Well, you've done most of the work. You can multiply twelve time eight."

By this time, Jennifer was around us showing me her completed problem and Gina has stopped crying. I remind her that she can do anything, and then remind both of the girls that they are smart.

In this case, the tutor simply broke down the multiplication problem for her tutee. But this act of understanding, and the fact that she was there to help, made all the difference to Gina.

Bargaining on the Relationship

Forming a friendship with your tutee allows you some influence over them. For instance, many tutors report how eager their tutees are to share good grades with them. Students want both to impress their tutors and to show that they are working hard in school. Once you have formed a relationship with a tutee, you can take advantage of these desires and make some demands upon them. Tutors are often surprised at how well this can work.

After three sessions in which this female Vietnamese tutor's Latino student forgot to bring his homework, she tried implementing a technique she had learned in an education class.

I turned to Gilbert and said, "You know, it's been three weeks and I have not been able to help you with your homework. Will you promise me that you'll bring your homework next week?"

He quickly responded with "Yes."

Somehow I was unconvinced. I continued, "And what if you forget to bring your homework? Do you know what's going to happen?" He was curious. I said, "I'm going to be really disappointed that you didn't keep your promise to me." He didn't say anything and returned to gluing tissue paper on his piñata.

After several minutes Gilbert asked, "What if I forget next week?"

I answered, "Then I'm going to be very disappointed."

This tutor didn't scold Gilbert. She didn't reprimand him or punish him. She used the trust that they had developed in their relationship; this technique wouldn't work between two strangers. But the tutor was pleasantly surprised when, one week later, Gilbert proudly pulled his homework from his backpack. Obviously, Gilbert cared enough not to let her down.

Setting Goals

We have stressed that tutors should avoid entering tutoring situations with preexisting expectations, *unfounded expectations* that can cause disappointment and erect a barrier between tutor and tutee. Once tutors have formed a relationship with their students and have some insight into their capabilities and how they are best motivated, they can begin to form *educated expectations*. Educated expectations are goals that tutors can set *with* their students. They are expectations that are ambitious yet realistic for the child, in the judgment of an informed mentor.

When tutees learn to trust their tutor, they can also learn to value their tutor's opinion. As that tutor, your opinions can have an important effect on a student's ambitions and motivations. The following example is from a tutor's experience with Ben, a sixteen-year-old high school student, who was doing a fair job but not excelling in any of his classes. When his tutor asked Ben about his grades, he replied that they were "good, I'm passing." The tutor encouraged him to work harder, citing his strength in math and suggesting he could probably get really good grades if he tried. Ben replied that his teacher had told him that if he did his homework he could probably get an A in the class, but he still resisted doing more work than was necessary.

It was obvious that he did not understand the benefit of getting good grades because he commented, "I don't see why I should do the homework if I know how to do the problems, and I am passing."

I found myself in unfamiliar territory. When I was younger, I did not understand the importance of homework either. I was the one who was always asking why I had to do my work, not the one explaining the importance of it. Luckily my parents were there to insist that I did it and explain why.

They had told me, as I in turn told Ben, "Homework is not the hardest thing to do in the world. But to master something, you need practice. Homework is like a way of practicing in order to master a subject. While the subject may have no real bearing on your life, an A in a class shows not only intellect, but self-discipline as well. Colleges are inundated with applications every year, and an important way to distinguish people is their grade point average, which is directly affected by doing homework."

Ben thought for a moment and then said, "Yeah, I never thought of it that way. I don't really like to do homework, but I guess I have to in order to be a [UCLA] Bruin."

His tutor's speech made an impact on Ben not only for that day, but for the rest of the time the two spent tutoring together. Ben continued to cite becoming a Bruin and going to UCLA as the reason he needed to work hard and finish his assignments. His tutor had become a guidance figure, someone that Ben could look up to and respect, and because of that relationship, the tutor was able to place these demands on his tutee.

A tutor can also use *educated expectations* to push students farther than they are at first willing to go. Goals are not always long-range. They can be immediate, as the following scenario demonstrates. The white female tutor knew that her Latina first grader was capable of sounding out words that she did not know but was re-fusing to exert the effort. Because they had been working together for several weeks and the tutor knew her capabilities, she made it clear to her tutee that they would in fact learn the trouble words, even if they had to dedicate extra time to it in future sessions. In this way she was able to motivate her student to try a little harder on the task at hand.

Estella was reading, pronouncing each word at a time, but whenever she got to the words *things, was where, were, there,* and *saw,* she had problems. "Sound the letters out," I told her. But rather than even trying she would look up at me and wait for me to start. I tried to explain about "*th*" and "*wh*" words, say-ing the sounds that they make, but it wasn't helping. Every time she got to one of those words she would immediately look at me as if to tell her what it was. "Remember, sound it out, that's the best way," I said.

"Sssss . . . aaaa . . . wwww," I tried to get her to sound it out with me, but either she was tired or she just didn't know, and I knew she knew.

She grabbed a piece of paper and wrote out each letter of the word so she would be able to sound it out. "w+h+a+t=what; w+i+t+h=with . . . " She did this with all of the words she was stuck on. But rather than having it help her, she began to get very distracted and anxious and was writing them very big on the paper and still asking me how to say it.

Then I noticed that some of the times she was looking at the picture to see if that helped her figure out what the word was. For instance, *things* became all the objects she could find in the picture on the same page, words which had none of the same letters.

"Where is the *d* in this word? Where is the *p*?" I felt bad, but I knew that she knew how to figure out what the words were. I told her to stop, and take a break because it was getting too difficult, and maybe she needed to rest her eyes.

I began to write down words she was not understanding, and she became very interested in them: "What are you writing?"

"I am writing down the words that you are having trouble with so next week I can bring them back and we can study them again; maybe I can make some flash cards." I could tell by the unhappy look on her face that this did not sound very appealing. And it was just then when she opened up her book and began reading again. This time she sounded out the words she did not recognize and got them, her speed and confidence level increased, and she raced through the sections. I had to stop her to tell her that she was reading the part she was supposed to read with her parents.

This tutor called her tutee's bluff. She knew Estella wasn't trying, so she explained to her that if she was having so much trouble reading, she would have to do some extra studying and maybe make flash cards for the words she didn't know. Faced with extra work, Estella was motivated to work harder at sounding out words. By learning what her student was capable of, this tutor was able to push Estella to work up to the *educated expectations* she had formed throughout their time together.

Going beyond Academics

Not only are tutors more effective by academic standards if they form a relationship with the tutee, but the relationship may also give them a chance to help the student with other problems. Teachers in a classroom of thirty rarely have time to deal with a student who appears troubled on any particular day. As a tutor with only a few students, you have the opportunity to lend some valuable support.

Ms. Lerder stood in front of the class and told them they only had a few more minutes to get their ideas together and finish everything up, so we began to focus back on the subject. It was good because Christine did not get a chance to speak yet. She was very quiet the whole time, and I asked her if anything was wrong. She said she was just having a bad day. Joanne responded by saying she always has a bad day. I quickly replied, "Maybe there is something really bothering her, Joanne."

I told Christine if she wanted to talk to me after class, I would. She said she didn't feel like talking about her legend and that she would do it on her own for homework. I asked if she had any ideas for homework. and she says she just wants to explain why it thunders. She did not sound happy. When we were walking out to lunch I talked to Christine and asked if there was anything I can do to help and just let her know someone cares.

Here, the tutor was able to venture outside her regular duties to provide some moral support for a problem that the teacher hadn't noticed and that Christine's peers dismissed.

For many students, tutors are mentors and role models. For others, they may be the only grown-ups whom the student can rely on or trust. Sometimes kids merely need to know that someone is genuinely interested in being involved in the activities of their lives. For this fifth-grade Latino student, having his tutor participate in his soccer game was highly important.

Desiring to have a good time and win the respect of Jason's peers on the field, I played hard while simultaneously trying to keep an eye on Jason. He was one of the least aggressive players on the team and rarely kicked the ball. He seemed almost to disappear out there among close to fifteen others his age. He never made a sound and didn't seem to be one of the more outgoing and well-known kids on his team. In fact, a couple of times when I passed by his area closely, he looked at me with delight that I was noticing him and tapping him. It seemed as though he felt special to have me out there with him even though I was playing against his team.

Tutors can also use their unique position in their tutees' lives to help fill them with confidence and new experiences. The following female Persian tutor was able to teach her male tutee, a new Persian immigrant, not only how to play basketball but how to interact with his peers and believe in himself.

Ahmed was standing in a corner of the playground all by himself. I called him over and asked him if he would like to play basketball with me. For a moment we was hesitant. Then he ran back to the classroom, grabbed a ball, and was ready to play. He dribbled down the court, went up and down the basketball court until he got tired, and stood next to the basket and he said that he does not know how. I asked him if he knew how to play; in response, he shook his head.

I explained the game to him. Then, we decided to play again. This time around, he actually knew what to do, but the game was a little boring with just the two of us. I could not help but notice Dylan and Joshua walking toward us. They approached us and asked if they could play. I said, "I don't know, Ahmed is in charge." They went up to him and asked him if they could play and since Aaron did not understand them, I translated for him. He smiled at them and said yes.

Once again Dylan teamed up with Joshua and Ahmed with me. Dylan named their team the Chicago Bulls and our team the Los Angeles Lakers. We began the game. Joshua passed the ball to Dylan and Dylan made a basket. Ahmed grabbed the ball, threw it at me and asked me to make a basket. Obviously, since I was taller then them, I was able to make a basket. Ahmed was filled with joy; he had a huge smile on his face.

Ahmed grabbed the ball again, threw it at me, and asked me to make a basket. However, this time I passed the ball back to him and asked him to make a basket. He stood there motionless for a while. He dribbled down the court and just stood right there. I was jumping up and down and telling him to shoot, but he would not. He yelled back at me, "I cannot do this! I don't know how."

From the look on his face, he was obviously frustrated. I really wanted him to make a basket. The only thing that seemed appropriate was to give him some words of encouragement. I yelled out, "You can do this. Just remember what I taught you!" Ahmed looked at the basket and then he looked at me. Allan yelled out, "Shoot already!" Well, what do you know, he made the basket.

Beyond this kind of moral support, a tutor can serve as a grown-up who cares, sometimes in stark contrast to the other adults that the student may meet in an overworked school system. One tutor was shocked when her tutee said that her teacher had told her she wasn't good enough to apply to the University of California (UC) system.

"So, did you get your UC application finished?"

Jessica said hesitantly, "Uh, no. I decided just to apply to private schools and Cal States. I just got lazy."

All at once I was upset, shocked, and saddened. She had worked hard on her essay and I had invested time in helping her improve it. "What do you mean, 'you got lazy'? You had an essay all ready to go."

"Yeah, but I talked to a teacher who told me that my SAT scores aren't good enough to go to a UC, and she said that maybe I should go to Cal State L.A."

"No, Veronica. You can go to a UC. You have to at least apply. You know you can do this. Do you have the application? We can fill it out right now."

"No, I got mad and tore it up."

"OK, when is it due, Friday?"

"No, Thursday."

"Well, can you get an application by tomorrow?"

"Yeah, I think so."

"I'm going to come back tomorrow at four o'clock and we will fill out a new application and send it off, okay?"

"Okay, Rebecca, I will do that."

In this case, Jessica's tutor knew that Jessica had a chance at the UC system because of some of the intense one-on-one work they had done together, She was able to apply this unique knowledge and encourage Jessica in directions she would otherwise have been forced to abandon. The votes of confidence and subtle pushes tutors can provide often make the biggest difference to the students.

Establishing Boundaries

With a strong tutor-tutee relationship, as with any relationship, come some problems. Tutors have to find their place on the relationship spectrum—somewhere short of an authority figure on the one end, and short of total and equal friendship on the other. It is a delicate balance that each student and tutor must negotiate. Personal issues sometimes threaten that balance, such as a student's jealousy of other students, tutees' overdependence on their tutor, and the ever-present possibility of separation.

Dealing with Jealousy

Once they have formed a particularly strong bond with a child, many tutors find that they have to deal with their student's jealousy. Such jealousy might focus on other students that the tutor works with, other aspects of the tutor's life, or other children or distractions in the tutoring site. As a tutor, you need to be aware of insecurity issues and how your behavior affects your students. But also be straight with them.

If you are working with several children in one classroom or station, it's your responsibility to make sure that all the children know that you are there for all of them but that they have to respect each other's time. Carefully but firmly, you can let them know that your working with another student in no way diminishes your friendship with them, but that they will have to wait their turn. Here is how one female tutor handled the jealous attachment of a nine-year-old Mexican American student.

> The other kids had already begun working on the second page of the worksheet [on why immigrants come into the United States], but Jade was stuck and asked me a question. "Why are new jobs a pull?" As I began explaining the reason, Kathy kept yelling, "Help! I need help! Help me." She was being really demanding and was just trying to be the center of the table's attention. "Why are you helping Jade? I want you to help me."
>
> I was sort of ignoring her because I thought that Jade needed my help. Kathy didn't like this at all and began to pout with her chin on the table between her clenched fists. She wouldn't answer any of my questions; I asked her, "Kathy, what's the matter? Is everything okay?" She wouldn't even look at me. I tried to explain to her that when we work in groups I need to be able to help everyone equally; I can't just concentrate on her. The period was over and it was time for me to leave. I said good-bye to the students and as I was leaving I looked at Kathy's desk; she didn't even turn around to wave a goodbye like she usually does.

Even though Kathy did not seem to accept having to share her tutor, by the next week she was eager and excited to see her. She was also much more gracious when her tutor explained that she would be spending some time with some other students.

Preventing Overdependence

Overdependence is another challenge that many tutors struggle with, especially tutors who get overinvolved in the lives of their students. There is a big difference between a healthy, temporary dependence and overdependence. Tutees need to depend on their tutor to gain the skills to make the jump to independence. But tutors often find it easy to fall into the Supertutor trap, in which they feel that not only can they help students in every aspect of their lives, but that it is their duty to do so. And, because tutors often act as role models for their students, students sometimes elevate them to idol status. This position creates a double bind for you as a tutor: a tutee may ask for help with a family or school problem, and it will be hard to deny this friend whom you feel has no other recourse. Remind yourself that there is no better way for a tutor to create an overdependent tutee than by stepping in and taking care of problems.

Solving students' problems for them can raise false expectations. This practice also increases their disappointment when they realize that their tutor is not infallible, or that they are not the main focus of the tutor's life. The following tutee, Justin, was a first grader who needed special help because he was being treated for cancer. Because he had been in and out of the hospital a lot, not only was he behind academically, but he had not learned to socialize with other children well. Justin invited his tutor to his home many times and she did visit once, even though the psychologist at Justin's elementary school had recommended against it. The tutor could tell that Justin came from a troubled family and that he felt neglected. Wanting only to make a positive impact on him in as many ways as possible, she may have created an unhealthy relationship.

At 4:25 P.M. Justin called and asked if I could come over and play. I was flattered but a bit uneasy, since the psychologist has asked me not to. I asked if his mom was there and I told her I am a tutor in Justin's class and that I live four doors down from them. I also informed her that Justin has asked me to come over several times, but when speaking to the school psychologist, we agreed that I talk with his parents first. She seemed delighted and told me that I was welcome to come over anytime this weekend. I told her I would come over tomorrow because I was on my way to work.

[The next day.] I came home and there was a message from Justin reminding me not to forget to come over. [I went over, met Justin's parents and played tetherball with Justin and his sister.] I hope Justin will not call too much and that he does not expect me to go over to his house too often. He is a nice kid and I want to help him, but I have many obligations and it will benefit both Justin and I when he makes more friends his own age.

[A week later.] Let's see, Justin has called twice today asking me to help with his homework or to play.

[The next day.] Justin called and asked me to come over to help him with his homework. "My mom and dad are not here, only the baby-sitter is here and she only does the dishes and cleans." I got the baby-sitter on the phone to ask her to help Justin. She handed the telephone back to him. "Oh, I forgot to tell you," he said. "The baby-sitter only speaks Spanish."

[A few days later.] As I was leaving, Justin grabbed my leg so I would not leave—it was like he dove to the floor and pulled it. Luckily I did not fall. I told him to get off but then Ms. Bowling intervened by raising her voice. He listened to her. I felt strange trying to discipline him, so I let her do it.

This tutor had only Justin's best interests at heart, but in thinking that she could make up for the attention Justin craved at home, she created not only an inconvenient situation for herself but a relationship in which a line had been crossed, and the process of defining boundaries with a demanding first grader became ambiguous. The tutor's other obligations made it impossible for Justin to be her first priority, but how was she to explain that to a child with whom she had worked so hard to build a strong, trusting relationship?

Justin also referred to his tutor as his "best friend" and preferred to play with her rather than with the other children at school. By allowing this, Justin's tutor reinforced his reluctance to form peer friendships. Rather than helping him, she inhibited the socialization process that he needed to learn, and his overdependence on her caused his further ostracism on the playground.

Children in need always want more of their tutors. Tutors need to be clear about what they are able and willing to give and do and what they cannot. Even though it is tempting to play hero to people you are helping, especially younger, troubled, or disadvantaged students, the greater gift is to allow them or help them learn to work out their problems on their own. For a temporary tutor to step in and solve things for them not only raises unrealistic expectations but robs them of learning this life skill. An overly dependent relationship also sets students up for a severe blow when the tutor must bow out.

The relationship you form with your student will be the basis of your tutoring, and the trust you build is exactly what makes the process more than just a passing on of knowledge or of techniques for passing tests. A tutoring experience can impact two or more lives for a lifetime—and that impact starts right there, in the relationship.

Recommended Reading

Tutors usually have a difficult time with the idea that rewards and gifts, no matter how small, can undermine the tutoring relationship. This is the result, undoubtedly, of growing up in classrooms in which rewards were used constantly. In public schools they received stickers, gold stars, edible treats, and awards. As they got older, they were perhaps placed on the honor roll, given special library privileges, and rewarded with money from their parents. No wonder many tutors have trouble accepting the idea that rewards are destructive.

But when one asks them how often they read books on their own; how often they have considered learning to speak a language outside of school language requirements; how often they have pursued interests that fall outside the domain of their education, they begin to see that they are motivated more by extrinsic rewards than by intrinsic motivation for learning. In "Stars and Bribes Forever" (1992) Joan Roemer has noted that all rewards have the same effect: they dilute the pure joy that comes from success itself.

No one, including children, needs a reward for learning, because the desire to learn is natural. This obvious and simple point deserves emphasizing. Just as adults who love their work invariably do a better job than adults who work for rewards, children are more likely to be optimal learners when they are interested in and fascinated by what they are learning than when they are merely striving for gold stars. Alfie Kohn, in a wonderful and wonderfully titled book, *Punished by Rewards* (1993), looks at why behaviorism with its emphasis upon rewards is ineffective in the workplace and at school. This book should be required reading for every educator, corporate executive, and parent.

The most destructive consequence of child rearing that links a child's performance to parental affection and love (rewards) has been described by Alice Miller in *The Drama of the Gifted Child* (1997). Miller calls "gifted" those children who are totally oriented toward figuring out what their parents, and later on their bosses and their mates, want. Once they have figured this out (because of their special ability to do this—their gift), they proceed to give the others what they want. This skill and ability is achieved at the expense of their developing a genuine self that can determine and respond to its own wishes, desires, values, and goals.

A number of studies have shown that students in the right environments can and do place more value on their actual education than on the rewards they receive from school or parents. For work that documents the ways in which college students sacrifice their own aspirations for learning, see *Making the Grade* (1968) by Howard Becker, Blanche Geer, and Everett C. Hughes. The authors' findings have been corroborated in "The GPA Perspective: Influences, Significance, and Sacrifices of Students" (1998) by Jerome Rabow, Hee-Jin Choi, and Darcy Purdy.

3
Teaching Techniques

One of the most remarkable things about tutoring is that in working with students one-on-one or even in small groups, tutors get to experiment in ways that few teachers have the time to. As a tutor, you have the opportunity to see how your students learn best and adapt your teaching to their learning styles. You have the chance to tailor your sessions to the exact needs of your student.

Although many tutors enter their tutoring situations somewhat bewildered and insecure about their teaching ability, after only a few sessions many come up with creative ways to teach and motivate their students. Methods vary, from games and hands-on programs to slowing down and reteaching concepts. No matter how or why teaching techniques are developed, their uniqueness is one of the best products of forming a strong relationship with your tutee; it demonstrates how important personal attention and understanding can be to the learning process. Tutors sometimes find that, with a little ingenuity, they can accomplish a lot in only a one-hour session.

All tutors discover particular teaching techniques that work with their own tutees. Just as every child and every tutor is different, so are solutions—there is no one, sure-fire solution to every problem. A suggestion from a friend or fellow tutor may work perfectly for you and your tutee—or it may fall flat. Something that you read here may seem like pure genius the night before a tutoring session, then provoke no reaction from your student.

The examples outlined here are not intended as templates for your tutoring sessions. There are no guarantees. But we have found a few guiding concepts that underlie most successful teaching techniques. We present them with a variety of examples that demonstrate another important aspect of tutoring: the creative process of basing your teaching methods on your unique insights into your tutees and their motivations and interests. In the examples, the tutors also draw on the strong tutoring relationship they have established with their tutees.

Often the best way to teach is to *get students involved and interested* in what they are doing. Students often approach learning (especially homework) with minimal motivation. They don't understand why they have to do the work or learn a particularly boring or difficult concept. The trick is to show the student that it doesn't have to be boring. Learning can be fun, and all subjects have some kind of application tutees can relate to. Finding something the student really enjoys and incorporating that into the lesson often takes imagination. How do you get a child who wants only to draw interested in math? In the answer to this question lies a solution to getting this student interested in learning.

In many cases, a student is reluctant to do schoolwork because it seems overwhelming or frightening. The first time students see algebra, the mixture of numbers and letters can be intimidating. The first time they deal with political concepts, they may find them too abstract to bother grasping firmly. In these cases, the first step is *easing the student's fear*. Once students are comfortable with a concept, they are much more willing to sit down and work. Try to make concepts less intimidating by relating them to concepts students have mastered, or by applying them to things they understand well already. A little familiarity can make a new subject seem much easier.

Something that frustrates many tutors is that students often don't do what the tutor would like them to. They don't pay attention well. They want to take breaks. Sometimes they aren't interested in a teaching method that a tutor has spent the past week developing. As a tutor, when students don't respond to your amazing idea of how to explain a subject or get them interested, you have to be willing to let it go. One of the most important aspects of tutoring is to *let students lead*. Even young children know what they are comfortable with and when they are ready to learn. Although you must exert some authority, when children show that they need a break or are leaning toward a particular learning style, follow them, even if it means giving up some of your own ideas about your teaching style. You will find that, given some autonomy, students will be much more responsive to learning.

Finally, *students like to be challenged*. Especially if you are working with children who have been labeled "slow," challenge is something school often offers them too little of. Many children and young adults may surprise you by rising to a challenge, even if the task is a bit daunting to them. Setting reasonable goals for students often proves an effective way to push them to make academic progress. The better your relationship with the student, the more effective challenges are. Students are motivated to meet goals that they formulate *with* people they like and respect. As your tutees struggle through these challenges, they satisfy your *educated expectations* of their potential.

Students are clever, and we will add a brief note at the end of this chapter concerning some common *techniques of students*. Having a tutor introduces the temptation of letting the grown-up do their homework for them. Although most students want help and are willing to do their own work, some will try to dupe tutors into doing their assignments for them. As a tutor, it's important not only to be aware of this temptation but to be firm with your students. The message you want to send is, you will help them with anything that they need help with, but you will not do their work for them.

The examples of teaching techniques that follow are specific, but the concepts behind them can be applied in any tutoring situation. In a strong tutoring relationship, many effective teaching techniques will seem to spring from the tutoring itself. Other techniques take a great deal of creativity, but activities and ideas that excite your student always exist. All you have to do is find them, put them together, and create your own techniques.

Getting Students Interested and Involved

The best way to get students to work, and work hard, is to get them involved and interested in the assignment—a simple goal not always easily accomplished. If the subject is a play or a novel or a history project on space exploration that the student is already moderately interested in, sometimes the excitement and enthusiasm of the tutor can motivate the student to get involved. With activities like math, however, it's often hard to get kids involved enough to pay attention and really want to understand concepts that are giving them trouble. It is the job of the tutor to make anything and everything of interest.

A multitude of possibilities exist. Sometimes it is merely a matter of *incorporating something that the student enjoys or is interested in* into the lesson, such as art or animals or sports. Other times, making the lesson a more *hands-on or visual experience* can grab a student's attention. Tutors have found that many students respond well to friendly *competition,* either with the tutor or with other students in the classroom or tutoring site. Such possibilities are endless, but they all mean getting the student (and yourself) involved in learning in ways that go beyond looking at a page in a book. Students respond best to dynamic learning, where they get to think and be creative.

Drawing on Student Interests

One of the best ways to motivate students is to incorporate their own interests into the learning experience. (We have said this before, and we will probably say it again.) A tutor needs to demonstrate how learning can help students do the things they want to do, and how to use their special talents and interests to help themselves learn. Tutors have found that they can use sports statistics to help teach math or an interest in clothes shopping and sales to help teach percentages. Tapping into a child's interest in art is also a popular way to make learning more fun.

This tutor found that his student Peter, an African American seventh grader, was often drawing when he was supposed to be doing his work. The tutor decided that Peter's interest in drawing might be the key to pulling him into other school activities and getting him personally involved in his math.

> I brought in an assignment to help Peter learn about fractions that incorporated his desire to practice drawing. I presented him with a list of objects found in a large broom closet (represented by a blank piece of paper). I told him that there were 24 items in all and that he had to figure out how many of the appropriate items to draw according to the clues. For example, one of the questions asked, "One-twelfth of the items are mini-monster guys." He figured out how much one-twelfth of 24 was and then proceeded to draw two of them on the sheet of paper. Even though he gave me a funny look when I was explaining the assignment to him, I could see that he enjoyed it and that it tested his knowledge of math while giving him the pleasure of showing off his drawing skills.

In the next example, the male Filipino tutor had a rough time interesting his student, a nine-year-old Latino, in reading. He found a solution by using both his own and his tutee's interests. During a session, the tutor happened upon his student's love of monsters and fantasies, which reminded him of the Filipino myths and folklore he had loved as a child. At the next session, he brought some related books for them to practice reading. This led to more reading and even enough interest to venture into the dictionary.

> Cristobal was fascinated at this world of giants and dwarves. He wanted to learn more and I felt successful in tapping some of the creative potential that I had seen earlier. He pointed to various legendary creatures, such as mermaids, the *aswong* or flying vampire, the witches, and each time I would explain it to him in the most provocative way I could. He liked the werewolf stories so he asked me to find something about it. I looked it up in a book and I helped him read about it. The reading was a little complex for his level, but I helped him along. Any words he did not know the meaning of, I asked him to look up in the dictionary.

Here the tutor not only got Cristobal interested enough to do a little extra research, reading, and work, but by sharing an important part of his culture, the tutor made the tutoring session and learning in general more fun, which is one of the main aims in tutoring.

Besides tapping into your students' interests, you can also get them involved in their assignments by drawing on their particular life experiences. As the next example demonstrates, teaching immigration terms to a fourth grader can be difficult, but they make a lot more sense when the student can apply the labels to his own family. This tutor found that baffling sociological terms became familiar to her fourth-grade Japanese American tutee when he could see how they related to himself and his parents.

> I went outside with Hiseo to work on the worksheet. I asked, "Are you an immigrant to the United States?"

He answered, "Yes. I mean, I think so. My parents came here from Japan."

I corrected, "Well, actually, your parents are immigrants, but you are not a first-generation immigrant like what we have been talking about. You were born in the United States, right?" He nodded in agreement. "Then you personally did not move here from another country, which constitutes the definition of immigrant, but you can be called a second-generation immigrant. Have you ever heard that before?"

Hiseo responded, "Yeah, I've heard the word but I didn't understand exactly what it meant 'til now. So I'm a second generation immigrant. Cool."

Relating learning to life experience also works with older students and much more complex topics and issues. In the following example, the tutor, a Filipina, found that her eleventh-grade African American female student who had been assigned to write a response to an article on affirmative action, a hot political topic at the time, was writing with a great deal of apathy. A little digging revealed that the student didn't understand affirmative action and was having a hard time putting the article in context and coming up with an informed response. The tutor framed her explanation in terms that directly related to both herself and the student.

> I tried to explain the idea in terms of something she could relate to. I said as a woman and a minority, I and yourself have been historically denied access to certain things. I told her that in jobs and in school, I would have never been given an opportunity to go to apply at a fire station. That I was not encouraged to apply because I probably would not get the job. With affirmative action, I was no longer denied but actually given the opportunity to apply for the job. I told her that minority women need to work harder in order to be at the same level playing fields as white males. After

we discussed the history of affirmative action, we read over the article again and she was able to respond to the article more thoroughly. Her response was much more thought out and coherent.

Other tutors have found it useful to incorporate current events or television shows that the students know a lot about. For instance, the O. J. Simpson trial was ideal for many comparisons, from defining vocabulary words such as *perjury* to explaining more detailed concepts such as the amendments to the U.S. Constitution, as this tutor did with her twelfth-grade student: "After finishing the reading, he told me that he did not understand it. I tried to explain everything by relating it to the O. J. Simpson trial and other things. This seemed to motivate him and I could tell he was beginning to comprehend the work. He noted, 'Hey, that is why Mark Fuhrman said he wanted to take the Fifth.'"

Switching roles with students to allow them to explore an unfamiliar job or position of power can also tap into enthusiasm. This female Mexican American tutor hit on a great technique with her sometimes troublesome African American fourth grader.

Today we worked on long division. I had tutored before and the teacher had told me that the best way to tutor was to ask the student to explain the material to you. This way you can find out what they know and what they do not. I did just that. I asked Terrence to explain the steps involved in dividing. I do not think he expected it, but he was excited about it. He looked at me with eyes wide open and asked, "So I'm the teacher?"

I said, "Yes."

He reacted by swinging his arm and yelling out, "Cool!" He seemed to enjoy this method because he smiled as we worked on the problems. He is very polite and conscientious about others. As he begins his explanation, he talks very slowly so I can understand. He also makes eye contact, especially after every step.

It's easy to see that the possibilities for getting students involved in their work are endless, as well as personal for each tutoring pair. The key is listening to students and remembering what they like and want to learn about. A big part of tutoring is making the relationship pay off for the students in greater understanding of their academic work and greater love for learning in general.

Making Work Visual and Hands-On

Visual effects can often invigorate boring work or highly abstract concepts, or at least bring them down to earth. Children respond to things that they can see and manipulate, so drawing and involving other physical objects in teaching often work well. Although these effects are particularly useful with young children, for whom visuals also help maintain attention, visuals can also help older students understand complex or hard-to-grasp concepts.

Effective drawings or diagrams range from simple charts or stick drawings to complex illustrations. Sometimes incorporating drawing turns work into play, in the student's eyes, as this white female tutor found with her stubborn seven-year-old Latina tutee, Elsa.

I tried to redirect her back to her schoolwork several times, but her attention span was fleeting and she continued to color. That was when I figured out how to get her to work without her knowing she was working. I took out a piece of construction paper and a marker, then wrote the word *perro* at the top of the page and *dog* underneath it. I then drew a picture of a dog beside these two words. "What does this say?" I asked her.

"D . . . aaawwwgg." We painfully sounded out each syllable, but this time she had more fun, because there was an illustration of the work there too. For every word or sentence I wrote in Spanish, I translated it in English underneath. This way she had to practice sounding out both languages. I wanted her to see the relation between words and meaning, so I made the sentences fairly self-explanatory—with a rather obvious picture below each one. This made the whole reading process less tedious for her.

In the next example, the tutor, a Latina, found that if she drew, turning the story she and her eleven-year-old Latina student were reading into a more visual experience, the student became more involved in the work.

I asked, "Do you want to take turns reading to each other?" She just sat there with a sad, blank face. So I decided to read the first paragraph. After I felt she was not listening and was not going to read, I began to draw out the paragraph on a white sheet of paper. When the history chapter talked about Magellan sailing on a ship across the Atlantic with all his men working hard to guide the ship through bad weather, I proceeded to draw a large ship, a strong man with a beard (who was Magellan), and all his crewmen on the ship. I made the waves of the Atlantic incredibly huge and drew rain coming down that looked like stormy weather. As I kept reading and drawing more pictures Carly began to get excited and she wanted to start reading and draw one paragraph.

The tutor in the following example found that giving her non-English-speaking Persian tutee something concrete to base his new knowledge on helped him to remember a letter that he was having a lot of trouble with.

Today was a great day, I finally did it. I helped Ahmed to remember the letter *m*. A classmate told me that it would be beneficial to relate the curriculum to things which he can relate to. For example, she mentioned that I should sing to Ahmed or bring toys or things to which he can relate. With that in mind, today before I went to tutoring, I stopped by Pavilions [a supermarket]. I went there to pick up a bag of M&Ms.

When I got to school, I asked Ahmed to write the letter *m*. Just as I expected, he had no clue. I reached for my bag, grabbed the box of M&Ms, and laid them on the table. I asked him what he called these colorful circles. He looked at me and thought I was crazy. He said, "M&M." I asked him, what did M&M start with? He opened up his eyes, put a smile on his face, and with a lot of confidence he said, "It starts with *m*." He asked me if he could have some, and I told him only if he promised not to ever forget that letter. He looked at me rather uncertainly and said, "Okay."

Another tutor, an Asian male, was frustrated even in his attempts to use drawings to explain the workings of the solar system to his student. He finally got the idea to use three-dimensional objects, which not only clarified the homework assignment to his student, a Latino fifth grader, but got him motivated enough to memorize almost all the material.

He whips out his ditto on the solar system. The student had to place the solar system in order, from Mercury to Pluto. Surprisingly, Guillermo doesn't know anything about planets. We try to memorize the order of the planets together but it goes slowly and I feel that Guillermo is not getting it. I attempt to draw them but that too is futile. By now both of us are hot and tired and I suggest that we step out for a bit.

With ditto in his hand, Guillermo and I trudge outside for some fresh air. As we are about to go back in, I spot a little girl playing with pebbles by the park. I suddenly get an idea to show Guillermo the solar system visually. "Hey, Guillermo, let's try to find stones that look like the planets."

For the next ten minutes we are bent over, searching for rocks. I come up with a large rock that is going to be our "sun" and a few stones that relate to the planets' sizes. Guillermo too comes to me with several stones. I am delighted to see a piece of brick which he tells me is Mars.

"All right! You knew that Mars was red!" I exclaim.

He replies, "Well, it says so on the ditto."

I can see that he is having fun. Now is it time for us to arrange the rocks in order. I place my "sun" stone in the middle and Guillermo proceeds to place the rocks using the ditto as our guide. We have to find a replacement for "Jupiter" though. Guillermo had brought a rock that was twice the size of the "sun." I place a string around the "Saturn" stone, representing the rings.

We take a step back to admire our own solar system and nod to each other. He still has a problem with Neptune and Uranus but other than that, this little dude definitely knows the solar system and also the relative sizes of the planets.

Encouraging Friendly Competition

Many tutors have found that a little friendly competition can help get students involved and interested in their homework. Even "boring" tasks like memorizing multiplication tables can become a game that kids enjoy and that excites them about learning. Tutors might make a Jeopardy! game out of math problems or facts from a history chapter. Scrabble and other learning games are also fun and effective for some students.

The Asian female tutor in the next example found that a game pitting her against her nine-year-old Latino student (putting them on equal ground, as far as the student was concerned) was the best way to help her student get his word search done.

After a while I didn't know what to do to help Esteban. So I decided to put a twist into his homework. I suggested that we have a race to see who could find the word first. He agreed and told me that he would find it first. We chose the word *America* and said, "Ready, set, go." I started from the top of the page and Esteban started from the bottom. I used my strategy and found it going across diagonally. "I found it," I said, kind of loudly. Esteban asked me where it was but I told him to look for it and I wasn't going to tell him right away. We kept racing and he found a lot of them first.

Competing with peers also often motivates students, and many tutors have a great deal of success using games to quiz kids for tests or on material they are supposed to memorize. This method can be especially useful when a group of tutees are all working on the same material, either in a classroom or at another common site. Again, something as simple as practicing for a spelling or vocabulary test can become fun and exciting—and encouraging. In the following example, the tutor found the method particularly successful in the fifth-grade classroom in which she was working.

I looked around the room and noticed a sense of curiosity from other children about what I was doing with Kevin and Mark. Soon a few students approached our table to see what we were doing. I explained to them that we were playing a game, a review game for the much anticipated vocabulary test. The students' eyes lit up immediately when I said the word "game." I incorporated the rest of the children into our intimate study group, and like the master of ceremonies at an awards banquet, I began the game.

I had Mark start, so he gave the group the first definition, "The bone that connects from the scapula to the ulna and radius." All the children thought about it as quickly as they could, feeling their bones, some at the scapula and some were feeling their ankles. I knew the results would be interesting when children were guessing bones all over their bodies. But in the end, some students came up with the correct answers.

Easing Student Fears

Although getting students involved in their studies is a great way to motivate them to work, and to want to work, some need more than motivation. Many students are reluctant to work because they are afraid of the material or intimidated by difficult concepts they have not encountered before. Even students who are generally motivated to learn can appear lazy or disinterested, when in fact they are hesitant to try an assignment they don't think they can succeed at. For these students, sometimes a lot of *support* will keep them encouraged enough to work on an assignment that intimidates them. Other times, *breaking the assignment down into small steps* that they are familiar with can be useful. Tutors also find success in *relating concepts to things that are familiar*—for example, families or a native language—to make strange concepts more comfortable.

Showing Support

Tutors may only need to offer a little encouragement and personal involvement to keep a student going through a difficult assignment. As with the following student, an assignment or task that seems difficult becomes possible if students know that someone is there to help if they need it. Not a strong reader, Jonah was hesitant to try to read aloud until the tutor provided moral support and the assurance that if he got stuck on a word, she would help him out.

> I asked Jonah to read. I got out of my chair and knelt down next to him and listened intently when he read. I helped him sound out almost every other word and little by little he was sounding

out the words alone. He was really struggling with pronunciation and his reading skills were that of a second or third grader. I proceeded to pat him on the back every time he made it through a sentence.

Breaking Assignments into Manageable Steps

A task like writing an entire sentence in cursive can seem impossible to a third grader just learning handwriting. In the next scenario, the tutor found that breaking the assignment down into individual letters helped a lot. She then tried to animate the activity for her student, to make it seem both more real and more interesting. This tutor found that adding a little fantasy to writing in cursive made it easier for her student to overcome her writer's block.

> Jenna was struggling to write a cursive *D*. "I can't do this letter. It's hard for me," she said.
>
> I told her that I knew she could do it and offered to show her how to do it. I took the pencil from her and said, "Okay, let's pretend the tip of the pencil is you sitting on a roller coaster. Okay, the roller coaster is going down the hill. All of a sudden, we come to a loop. Let's follow the loop all the way up and we hit another loop. What does that look like?" I asked.
>
> "A *D*," Jenna responded. She took her pencil and repeated the exercise again.

In the following case, the concept of syllables seemed like nuclear physics to the nine-year-old, third-grade Latino tutee. His tutor, an Asian female, found that all she had to do to make the concept manageable was introduce something familiar to the foreign concept. She found that syllables were a difficult concept to grasp that became easier with names that were close to home.

After finishing the first worksheet we moved on to the second worksheet, *Syllables*. I asked him if he knew what a syllable was. He told me no. I said his name, Tomas, while clapping, To-mas. "How many different sounds do you hear?"

He said, "Five."

"Five? Why do you hear five?"

He said, "Because there are five letters."

I told him to try not to think about how many letters were in a word. Then I asked him how many brothers and sisters he has. He told me three. Two brothers and one sister. His sister is ten and his brothers are three and nine months. Then I asked him what their names were. We went through all his siblings' names and talked about how many syllables each one has.

Tying in Familiar Concepts

Often just a little simplification or familiarization can help students get over their fear of an assignment and get started; then they can see for themselves just how capable they are. This technique can also be useful when dealing with students for whom English is a second language. Tutors who speak their student's native language, however poorly, often find the ability helpful. Some tutors, like the one in the following example, draw on a relatively limited knowledge of the student's native language to help make some connections. Here, a Latina tutor was able to help her nine-year-old tutee, who was also Latino.

Again he used the glossary in the back of the book, but I could tell that he did not know the difference between a verb and a noun. I defined noun as "a person, place, or thing" and a verb as an "action word." I thought that this definition was inadequate and unclear, so I thought that I would relate it in his first language of Spanish. I told him that a verb "was like *leer* in

Spanish, which means 'to read.'" I asked him if he understood a little bit better and if he could tell me another example. He cited the word *correr,* which means "to run" in Spanish.

By using examples of Spanish terms with which the student was readily familiar, this tutor found that explanations about English equivalents became much more solid and understandable for the student.

Sometimes students hesitate to get involved in assignments or learning activities because they get frustrated or are afraid that they won't do well. In the next example, the tutor found that bilingual Scrabble was a good way to get her fifth-grade Latino students involved in vocabulary and spelling, but one of the students, an "English as a second language" (ESL) student named Jimmy, got embarrassed while playing. Afraid that Jimmy would not want to continue playing, the tutor instituted a rule that took into consideration something that Jimmy excelled at. She found that this new rule kept Jimmy's morale up and encouraged him to keep trying.

When he was done he put the paper away and went to get Scrabble. As we got out the game, Jimmy came in early. I asked him to join us and he shrugged and sat down. We were all on separate teams.

During the course of the game, Jimmy really struggled with the concept. He would make a word with his letters without incorporating any of the letters on the board. He made the word *dog* and put it on the board without connecting it with any other letters. I asked him to try and find a spot for the word. He found an *o* on the board and placed it with those letters. I was really happy when he got the concept, but the word *dog* had another word directly underneath it vertically and the letters going vertically didn't make a word. I didn't know how to break it to Jimmy because he looked so happy. Pedro told him in Spanish and Jimmy took his word off the board.

It was clear that Pedro understood the game much more than Jimmy, and I didn't want to offer my help to Jimmy because he might feel stupid when Pedro didn't need any help. Jimmy is very good in Spanish so I invented a new rule. I told them that when a word in English was put down on the board, the first one to say what the word was in Spanish would earn an extra point. Jimmy really got into this new rule. Although he was still having a tough time coming up with his own words, every time a word was put down he would shout out the word in Spanish. He earned a lot of points this way. His interest in the game also increased.

Tutors who are tuned in to their students usually know when they are scared of the material. Such fear can be crippling for the student and frustrating for the tutor. But sometimes all it takes to allay fears is bringing the activity closer to home or incorporating something that the student already excels at. Students can often break down and understand concepts that at first seem complex and intimidating—with a little help.

Letting the Student Lead

Some tutors go into a session with a lesson in mind and plan far enough ahead to bring along props and materials, but lessons are often ad hoc, and tutors make do with the materials at hand. This situation, however, is not always a handicap. Tutoring sessions often happen in libraries, a rich resource for research on any subject that may interest a student. Classrooms and tutoring centers will often offer up something to use for an activity or interesting reading for a student. One of the greatest advantages of a little adlibbing in a tutoring session is that it allows the students a chance to tell the tutor where they want the session to go and how they want to work.

When you tutor, both you and the students need to know that

the tutor is in charge and that all of you are there to get some work done. Yet children often work best when they have some autonomy over their tutoring sessions. Students themselves can often give you some idea of how they learn best, or at least how they will learn best at any particular moment. A way to let students lead is to give them some choice about how they will learn and how long their learning periods will last. As you *listen to your students*, you can learn a great deal about their interests and their attention spans. You can also *be sensitive to how children aren't learning*. When techniques that you think ought to work don't, you can be alert and willing to change tactics.

Judging when to lead students, when to follow them, and when to get out of their way will be an ongoing challenge. But you will find that as time passes, you will understand what makes your tutees work, and as you do, your relationship will begin to lead the tutoring sessions naturally. Because you will get to know your students both personally and academically, your *teaching techniques will develop as you tutor*. The more time you spend with students, the better you will be able to adapt your style and add new and personal teaching techniques.

Listening to Students

Many students, especially those who have worked with tutors before, have some idea of how they like to learn. As great as it is to introduce them to new techniques and to be creative, it's just as important to listen to them. The tutor in the following case not only used the suggestion of her five-year-old Latina tutee, but also creatively incorporated her surroundings to create an active learning experience.

The director tells us we can work on letters and numbers or some coloring, so I lead Elsa to the area where there are crayons and games. I search through the container for some crayons, but I can't find any that we could use. But Elsa picks out some flashcards with letters and a picture that begins with a specific letter on each card. I then lead Elsa off to the side, where there are blocks and other toys. Meanwhile I am trying to think of how I can use the cards. I then noticed that the carpet had the alphabet written around its edges, so I decided that I could have Elsa place each card on top of the correct letter.

An important part of being a successful tutor is taking advantage of the materials and opportunities around you to make learning fun and interesting, both for you and for the student.

Another tutor who worked with Elsa found that she had to be creative to work around her tutee's relatively short attention span.

In her backpack there was a book, *Mi Sonrisa y Yo*. We started going through the easy reader together. Elsa must have read this book several times before, because she clearly knew a couple of the lines by heart. I originally wanted her to attempt every word before I helped her, but this method was much too frustrating for her. She was up and about, switching chairs and dancing around mine. It was impossible to keep her focused.

When I realized how short her attention span was and how quickly she gave up when frustrated, I began doing more of the initial reading myself and allowing her to repeat after me. Although I think that the learning environment would have been more ideal if she did all of the reading on her own, I do not realistically think we would have been able to make it past the first page that way. When I read the words aloud first, she could still practice reading and seeing how the individual letters made sounds, but she could also grasp the meaning of the story as a whole.

This tutor had to be flexible. That she was able to adjust to her student's learning habits made it possible for them to accomplish some reading instead of frustrating each other.

Letting your students lead may also mean letting them work on what they want to work on —what interests them. Doing schoolwork with tutees is a big part of tutoring, yet it's also important to encourage students to explore their own ideas. In the next example, the female Asian tutor found that her two fourth-grade students were more interested in Shakespeare than in social studies.

Gillian, Toni, and I went to the auditorium, where there were several tables and chairs set up. After we sat down, Toni said, "Let's read *Romeo and Juliet!* I have the book right here." Toni showed me a small, soft-covered copy of the play.

I asked, "Whose book is this? Is it yours?"

Toni replied, "Oh, I brought it from home." She then pleaded, "Please, please, can we read this book?" I promised her that we would read some after we read some pages in the social studies book that Ms. Lerder wanted us to read from. Toni pleasantly agreed to my plan.

Toni and Gillian took turns reading from the book that described the transcontinental railroad. They both read with fluency and ease. They took turns reading a paragraph each and I was pleased by their enthusiasm to read.

After we finished reading one of the sections in the social studies book, I told the girls that they could read *Romeo and Juliet*. Toni became very enthusiastic then; she gently yelled, "Yay!" then immediately began to flip through her book, looking for the best parts to act out.

Gillian and Toni had fun acting out their parts, especially the sword fighting. Whenever one person was reading their line (there was only one copy of the book), the other person would pretend to jab the reader with a sword. The two girls almost continually giggled and laughed. They had trouble pronouncing many of the words, and they read much slower then when they read the social studies, probably because the sentence structure was unfamiliar. I knew that they were having trouble understanding what they were saying to each other, but they still enjoyed it.

When Toni read a line, "Do you bite your thumb at me?" she literally began biting her thumb in front of Gillian. Gillian followed and bit her thumb as well. They laughed while doing this and I did too. I explained to Toni that what she read actually meant "Are you insulting me?" She then understood and both girls stopped biting their thumbs, but they still giggled and laughed as they read their parts.

Even though the Shakespeare and its concepts were difficult, the girls were involved in their reading and having fun, one of the best aspects of learning that tutoring can introduce students to. They challenged themselves and introduced themselves to one of the great writers of the English language, all on their own initiative. All the tutor had to do was let them enjoy reading it—and do some translating.

Sometimes the best teaching techniques have more to do with organizing and arranging the session and motivating the students than with actually teaching them. Most tutoring sessions come after a full day of school for the students, when motivation may be at its lowest. Many tutors feel guilty if they do not use every moment of tutoring time to be productive, but sometimes a break can do more good than harm.

In the next case, the tutor found that breaking up the session helped his student, a fifth-grade Latino, concentrate longer: "It took no longer than twelve to fifteen minutes before I could tell that I was losing his interest. Therefore I offered him a backyard break when he got to a certain place in the homework. He plugged along as normal until about 5:20, then we headed outside to get a breather before returning to homework."

By paying attention to what a student likes, you may even be able to establish study breaks that are not only fun but constructive: "Gus suggested, 'Let's read another one of those stories like we did last week when we're done.'

"I agreed. I was thrilled because I had a great time reading them too. I said, 'Great idea, that was so much fun, let's hope we have time.'"

Having something fun to do at the end of a session can be a real motivator, helping students concentrate harder and work more efficiently. The anticipation also gives the session a tone of fun rather than of simply work.

Looking at What's Not Working

Just how far to push a learning situation is another issue tutors deal with. How much help is too much? How much pushing is too much? At what point does the session go from fun to boring to downright tedious? All tutors and students have to push and experiment with these boundaries. In the following instance, the tutor found both successes and failures in her first session with her student, a Latino fifth grader, but the entire experience helped her establish where to go next.

As we began to read, I realized the extent of his problem, for he did struggle with pronunciation. Rather than decreasing his motivation by continually correcting him, I allowed him to break down each syllable to figure out the pronunciation on his own. Only when he asked, "What's this word?" did I help him. I also told Sam to ask me for explanations if he had trouble understanding the meaning of any word. He quickly nodded.

Whenever he had difficulty reading a certain word, I asked him whether he understood the meaning. He answered, "No." I wondered why he didn't ask me. As we read further, I realized that he did not understand a lot of the words; therefore, I suggested that he write those words down and look them up in the dictionary. He quickly whined, "Naaah, that's so boring! Why do we have to do that? I just want to read." I tried to explain that it's important to learn the meanings of words, and he reluctantly agreed.

Having pondered it, I regret forcing him to use the dictionary. Not only did this process break the flow of the story, but I created a boring environment that is not conducive to learning. Sam was bored and probably didn't care to learn the words at that particular time.

Adjusting as You Go

One of the most exciting things about establishing an ongoing relationship with your students is that, as time passes, your techniques usually improve and you adapt them better to each tutee. In the dictionary case just quoted, the tutor learned quickly that her student had a short attention span and that she needed to work to keep him interested. As this same tutor-student team continued to work together, the tutor found other ways to break up the session to make it more fun and to encourage Sam to work harder.

Throughout the session, as he got problems right, I would tell him to take a bow as he did. He got a half bow when he completed every question and full bow when he finished every third question. He liked this a lot and enjoyed the physical comedy he could display with such self-approval that I have got to admit it was fun.

When the bowing wore thin, we tried a little missile-launch practice. As we took about a ten-minute diversion from the problems themselves to just focus on the multiplication table, I would make a hit sound (like a siren) when he got problems correct and a miss sound (like the error buzzer on a game show) when he didn't. This went over well as we enjoyed ourselves and gave Sam a greater desire to struggle with the material and remember the ones we have been going over that he didn't know well.

Often as you work with students over a period of time and get to know them better, you can employ a variety of techniques to challenge them in different ways. In the next example, the female tutor found her third-grade Latina student willing to work hard but lacking confidence. To address this issue, she changed her techniques, even though her former techniques had been fairly useful in teaching multiplication.

My fourth week at Mar Vista began with Claudia arriving on time and with one assignment for homework. As usual, the assignment was a multiplication worksheet. A recurring thing I notice in my time with Claudia in terms of her math work is she always looks to me for the answers or approval of her results. I am still trying to help her realize that she must learn to trust herself and her abilities. . . . Now before I would watch her do every problem and work with her on each one. If she would answer the problem, she would look to me for approval or correction. . . .

Today I tried to do something a little different. She pulled out the infamous multiplication worksheet. and she started on the first problem. I told her, "Claudia, let's try it this way. Finish the worksheet, don't worry about the problems you don't understand or aren't able to get because we'll work on them together. But this time I won't hover over you and I won't help you . . . yet. You know the answers and I know you can find them. . . ." I ended with, " I know you can do it, Claudia."

The sheet was about forty problems, and she finished in about ten minutes. She skipped seven of them and, when I looked at it, of those done only about four or five were wrong. I worked on those problems with her, using the "walking" through method. We completed the assignment in about half an hour.

With this new technique, Claudia's tutor not only showed her how to multiply, but proved to her that she was learning to do it on her own.

Challenging Students

One of the best things a tutor can do is challenge students in a way they'll enjoy. You are there both to engage and interest them in learn-ing and to challenge them to learn more. You can challenge them in small, immediate steps, such as daring them to learn a spelling word. Or you can give them longer-range goals, such as improving a grade in a class or getting a good score on a test that is coming up. Other challenges are even more far-reaching, such as being a good, moti-vated student or sticking to a goal, such as applying to college.

Sometimes a simple challenge is effective. In the following case, a second grader had been assigned to use vocabulary words in sen-tences. This simple activity turned into something more exciting and personal for the child with a few queries from the tutor.

"How can you use 'grow' in a sentence?"

He thought about it and quickly came up with, "The cow grows."

Although this sentence is grammatically correct, I have seen him come up with better examples. This simple sentence simply reflects William's desire to rush through the homework and does not demonstrate his application of creative thought process. Therefore, I challenged him, "Hmmmm, 'grow' can be used in so many ways! Can't you expand your sentence?"

He looked at me blankly, and I knew I had to urge him further. "Okay, William, think about this. What would you like to be when you 'grow' up? A soccer player, a baseball player, a fireman?" I encouraged him to think more analytically by offering him several options.

He began slowly, "When I grow up I want to be . . . a coach for a baseball team."

You can also challenge students to take pride in their work. Too often they turn in homework without rechecking it for correctness; students are reluctant to put in extra effort to make their work good. But a creative tutor can find ways to make extra effort worthwhile. In the next instance, the tutor found that making accuracy a game compelled his student, a ten-year-old Latino, to take pride in his work and be willing to check his answers.

I wanted to teach him a skill that he could take with him. I taught him how to check the answers of his problems to guarantee an A+ on all of his math problems. I showed him how to take the answer and plug it into the problem to see if it works. I showed him how to do it and then asked him if he would like to check all the problems. He replied, "No." I then decided to make a bet with him and try to make math fun. I told him that if I checked a problem and if it was wrong, then we would have to check all the problems, and if he was right then we could play any game he wanted. He won.

Besides challenging their students, tutors have an equal obligation to allow the students to challenge themselves. The white female tutor in the next scenario had been working with her fifth-grade Latino student, Miguel, for several weeks, when she realized that she might not always be pushing him to push himself. Miguel was considered a troubled child and often labeled as unmotivated and disruptive, labels that the tutor tried to ignore and even combat. In this instance, however, she found that even she fell into the labeling trap sometimes, failing to treat Miguel as a student who might want to go above and beyond the assignment.

> I allowed Miguel to have a few minutes to work on his own, and then I went over to see how he was doing. I noticed that he was cutting out portions of articles, and so far only two articles. I explained to him that he needed to cut out single words from the newspaper. He seemed to immediately understand. He said, "Oh!" threw away what he had already cut out and quickly began cutting out single words he could use [in the poetry he was supposed to write with them].
>
> I realized that he had not understood Mr. Arnold's directions, but now that he did, he was right on task. Miguel had received the Calendar section of the L.A. *Times,* so he was finding many movie titles and entertainment-related words. He began to cut out the word *neurosis.*
>
> I told him, "I think that word is going to be difficult to put in a poem, maybe you shouldn't cut it out."
>
> "It's okay," he said.
>
> "Do you know what it means?" I asked.
>
> "No," he said.
>
> "Well, Mr. Arnold said that you should only cut out words that you know the meaning of, because you're going to have to use them in your poetry," I said.
>
> Miguel looked at me with a "duh" kind of look on his face, "I'll just look it up!"
>
> A little embarrassed that I had not suggested that, I said, "That's a really good idea." And I handed him the dictionary.

Recognizing Student Ploys

Many students are extremely adept at convincing tutors to do their work for them. The tutor is there to aid the student, and prompting a student toward a right answer, for example, falls within that definition; filling in answers or writing a paper for a student does not. Tutors sometimes find that they are being manipulated by their students. As in the following case involving a male fifth-grade Italian student and a female tutor, this realization often doesn't come until after they have been tutoring the child for a while.

> He was completely aware of how much work we had ahead of us. Let me rephrase that, how much work he had ahead of him. Sometimes I feel like Terry pretends he does not understand an assignment, when he really is trying to get me to give him the answers. He does it subtly, of course, for example, if Terry doesn't know what a word means or how to spell it, he'll ask me instead of looking it up in the dictionary.

Other students will frankly ask a tutor to do work for them. In these cases, no matter how unsettling the situation may be, it's important to lay down your guidelines right from the start. Set the tone for your tutoring sessions from the first session by being positive yet firm. The tutor in the next example found that, with a little friendly pressure, his tenth-grade student was willing to work.

> Mike pulled out his science book and said, "Will you help me make an outline on photosynthesis?"
>
> "Sure. Let's start by writing down some facts about photosynthesis. Why don't you tell me what you know about it?"
>
> He began to laugh again and said, "That's the problem that I need help with. I don't know anything about it."

I asked, "Mike, what chapter in your book is photosynthe-
sis discussed?"

He replied, "Chapter four, I think."

I countered, "Have you read it?"

He said, "No."

I couldn't believe he was asking me to explain something in
order to avoid reading the material himself. I said, "I'll make
you a deal. Why don't you read the chapter right now and af-
terwards I will answer any questions you have."

"Oh, man, all right."

To give a tutee the answer may be tempting. Tutors get tired and
frustrated too. But to make students do the work is to make them
learn. In the next case, the Latina tutor felt frustrated with her
nineteen-year-old Latino student but resisted both her student's
pleas and her own inclination to give up.

Jorge was not familiar with any of these words so I told him to
look them up. He referred to the page that contained the defi-
nitions of each of the terms, yet he could not figure out which
word belonged in the context. He didn't seem to know the difference between a verb and an adjective. There was a section of
the worksheet that required filling in the blank with the right
vocabulary word.

I tried to show him a clue that would hint the right answer
by figuring out what part of speech was missing. For example, if
the sentence read, "The teacher did not want to _____ his
students with too much homework," I showed him that the
word "to" hinted that the blank must be a verb, so we could narrow down the words on the list to verbs only. When I asked if
he knew what I was talking about he said, "Yes." But when I
asked him to do the next problem on his own, he couldn't figure
it out.

He kept saying, "C'mon, just help me out. What's the answer?"

"Nah, I can't just tell you the answers. Look it up. I know you can figure it out." Despite my encouragement, he did not do the work without my help. For each of the next eight sentences, I would have to guide him through it, figure out the part of speech of the missing word, and narrow down the choices on the list, so he could write the one that fit the context. We finally finished the worksheet, but definitely not without being tempted to just tell him the answer.

By not giving her student the answers and patiently walking him through each step that she used to find the correct word, this tutor may have still been doing some of her student's work. But in the process, the tutor was passing on the tools that she herself uses to do her own work to a student who hadn't learned them. This is knowledge he would have been cheated of if she had just handed him the answers.

As we've seen, an activity such as looking up words in the dictionary can either encourage or discourage hard work. So there is no fast rule about what students should be helped with and what they should be left to do on their own. But, as Mike's tutor did, you'll realize that even good kids sometimes try to get away with doing as little work as possible. The key is staying aware and, no matter how anxious you are to help, making sure that your students are doing their own work and learning along the way.

Building on the ideas in this chapter, you'll discover many ways to convince your students that not only can they do the work, but they can enjoy themselves and excel at it. Go into your sessions with an open mind, plan to be creative, and maintain a keen eye for what your student gets excited about. One of the main objectives of tutoring is to encourage your students to continue to learn and succeed in school after your relationship has ended. To this end, making learning fun becomes one of a tutor's greatest achievements.

Most of the tutor behaviors that we have encouraged in this chapter neither replicate nor reproduce the patterns of learning and responding common in traditional U.S. classrooms. Our tutors' successful teaching techniques emphasize (1) active learning, with all the noise and movement of students doing, talking, collaborating, experimenting, and experiencing hands-on that go along with it; (2) higher-order thinking rather than rote memorization; (3) choices for students (in terms of book and activity selection); and (4) more cooperative and collaborative activities for students, both with their tutor and with their peers. Techniques that fall within these guidelines often succeed in exciting ways, even for children who have failed to thrive in regular classrooms. In this sense tutors are educational reformers. Every new, exciting, and unique technique that you develop enriches the education of your students.

Recommended Reading

The attention you pay to your tutees, their needs, and the teaching style that works best for them is often an antidote to the contention by many critics of contemporary education that children find school boring and purposeless. In *A Place Called School* (1984), John Goodlad documents the efforts of secondary school teachers to keep students under control and passive. This repression of spirit and curiosity occurs just when adolescents need to be taking control of their education. Goodlad shows that, by taking them through rote exercises and tedious busywork, our education system often teaches children to give back the "standard" answers rather than to learn and speak on their own.

Through his work with adult students, Paulo Freire challenges the traditional model of teaching in which the teacher is the source of all knowledge and the student merely a passive recipient of this knowledge. In *Pedagogy of the Oppressed* (1989), he develops an active learning model in which students learn to take control of their own education.

For a wonderful compilation of active learning practices in teaching a range of school subjects, from reading and writing to math and science, see *Best Practices: New Standards for Teaching and Learning in America's Schools* (1995) by Steven Zemelman, Harvey Daniels, and Arthur Hyde. Not only do the authors put together specific techniques to engagingly teach specific subjects, the book includes a number of general pointers that should prove key to any tutoring partnership, such as less memorization of facts and details; less time devoted to dittos, workbooks, and "seatwork"; more experiential, hands-on learning; and more emphasis on higher-order thinking.

4
Race, Gender, Class, and Background Differences

As you can see, forming a close relationship with tutees and becoming a part of their world are essential steps in creating a successful tutoring partnership. Not only does a close relationship give you as the tutor access to ways to motivate and interest your student, but your most successful teaching techniques will stem from that relationship. As you have surely anticipated, however, many factors can inhibit a strong tutor-tutee relationship.

Among these factors are the expectations and anxieties tutors and tutees bring into the relationship. Tutoring is easiest and most beneficial for both parties when those expectations and anxieties can be left at the door (see Chapter 1). But many such feelings stem from a common and real fact of tutoring: often the tutor and the tutee come from drastically different backgrounds. Many tutors find themselves working with a student of a different gender, race, age, class background, or sexual orientation. Often the everyday world of the tutee is one the tutor sees only on the evening news.

Ideally, tutors easily overcome these factors. We are all people; tutors, driven by the desire to help, should not be hampered by these differences, right? But such differences are real and sometimes startling. Tutors who find themselves working with children and adults who do not speak English well are often frustrated because they do not know the students' native languages. Tutees have approached their tutors to ask for help with a gang problem, and the tutors have had no idea what advice is appropriate. Sometimes the discomfort a thirteen-year-old boy feels about opening up to his female tutor can create a substantial barrier to tutoring. In expressing her relief at her own tutoring situation, the following Latina tutor sums up the fears of many new tutors:

> There were three things about Janie that eased my nervousness about tutoring. First, she welcomed me warmly, with a gentle smile. Her familiarity with the tutoring process made it evident that she must have had a couple of tutors before. Secondly, at the risk of sounding sexist, she was female. The fact that she was a girl, instead of a boy make me think that tutoring would not be as stressful, because I was under the assumption that boys were harder to control. Thirdly, Janie was a Spanish speaker. I assumed that because we had language and ethnicity in common that would facilitate my tutoring.

Just as it seems natural to be relieved that you have a lot in common with your student, it's quite understandable for differences to make tutors somewhat uncomfortable.

Before tutoring has even begun, differences can create major barriers to the formation of a relationship (see Chapter 1).[1] Some tutors start to imagine the differences between themselves and their tutees from the moment they read a description of their tutoring

---

[1]Throughout this chapter we will refer to students and tutors who are *different* from one another. We use the term to refer to tutors or students who are of a different gender, age, race, ethnicity, religion, class, social background, or sexual orientation from the person with whom they are working in the tutoring situation.

site or hear about others' tutoring experiences. Other tutors are struck by just how far their world is from that of their tutee when they first arrive at the site or meet their student.

Issues of difference also arise *throughout the tutoring relationship*. As a tutor, even after you form a relationship with a student, your contrasting backgrounds are bound to trigger some interesting conversations and probably a few missteps by both you and the tutee. We all hold assumptions and have our own versions of reality. Your versions will sometimes clash with your tutees', when they hold different assumptions and life-world views. Sometimes students will show their discomfort with you, and other times your differences will become obvious when you say something that students either don't understand or consider inappropriate. At still other times, your differences will appear when you feel it is especially important for you to understand— when your student trusts you enough to come to you with a problem.

Although these incidents often create moments of discomfort, frustration, and sometimes distress, most differences are not insurmountable. Adopting many of the attitudes outlined in Chapter 1, you can *work around and overcome these differences* to form relationships with students of radically different backgrounds than your own. All tutors can work to minimize the differences and develop the common ground between themselves and their students, and, as the relationship develops, come to accept the differences. In the end, the differences in background and culture can themselves contribute to making the relationship a most rewarding learning experience for both tutor and tutee.

Anticipating Differences before the Relationship Begins

Fears about tutoring can be crippling, even before the tutoring encounter takes place. Throughout the United States, tutors— often university students or people from the upper middle class—

are volunteering in inner cities and with prisoners, immigrants, homeless people, and many others with whom they might feel less than comfortable in an everyday encounter. Tutoring often brings tutors into neighborhoods and social situations they could not imagine themselves in for any other reason.

Tutors may erect mental barriers based on their *fears* regarding a particular site. Such fears resemble the general fears discussed in the first chapter, yet they may be even more potent when they spring from information about the tutoring site. As you prepare to tutor, the limited information that you receive about your site before you go may be enough to evoke a fair amount of fear specifically related to the students you will be tutoring.

Differences between the tutor's and the tutee's background may become starkly apparent when the tutor first arrives at the site or meets the tutee. It is hard not to form opinions upon these *first impressions*, and in many cases, a spur-of-the-moment impression will leap to mind—"Oh my gosh, this child is dirty. His family must not take care of him." These first thoughts may create an obstacle to the formation of a strong relationship.

Organizational factors or pressures at the tutoring site can sometimes aggravate the differences between tutors and tutees. Some site directors have preferences that are implied in their pairing of tutors and tutees. Some sites seems designed to serve only a particular ethnic group, which can make tutors of other races or ethnicities ill at ease.

Quieting Presite Fears

When tutors set out on the adventure of tutoring, they are usually equipped with little accurate information about the tutoring site or tutees. If they know anything about their site, it is usually minimal and often not reassuring. To know that the tutoring population is all minority, non-English speaking, or poor can be disconcerting for a middle-class tutor who doesn't normally interact with a diverse group of people. As politically correct as our society has become, it's naive to think that stereotypes, prejudices, and fears have disappeared. Many people who volunteer to tutor have had little contact with the communities they want to help.

That this ignorance can be unnerving is reflected in the following tutor's candid notes: "I was scared of 'retarded' people. I'm afraid of black people. I do not fear them personally, but I fear my inability to share and relate as fully as I can to people who have had similar life experiences. In writing this I feel a great deal of discomfort and guilt. I feel like it sounds prejudiced, or as if I think I am qualitatively better than black people. I do not believe that I feel this way. So here I am."

Feelings like these are hard to express, and many tutors leave them bottled up inside. As much as these emotions are socially unacceptable, they are real, and tutors need to be honest with themselves, know what their fears are, and work to overcome them. If they don't, their tutees will often sense that something is holding their tutor back. Tutees are astute, as the following tutor, who was examining her own fears and anxieties, was aware: "Would I be rejected as a white poseur trying to invade this community thinking I was the only way to help the kids here to get the socially defined goal of college? I was suddenly aware of my face, my clothing, my posture. I felt like my smile was fake. It is one of the worst feelings in the world, and people can read it on you—fear and insecurity."

Many tutors opt for sites at which they feel they can make the biggest impact. Sometimes it is exactly these sites that evoke the most anxiety in the days or hours before the first session. The following comments come from a white female who had signed up to tutor in a program for high school-age students who had qualified for early parole, most of whom were still on house arrest and whose crimes ranged from robbery to assault and battery to murder.

I met the organizer of the program in their main office in [a middle-class/poor African American neighborhood]. She was really positive and really excited about the program which made me feel really good. But the tutoring is actually going to take place deep in the heart of South Los Angeles, in an area I've never even driven through before.

Amy [the director] says that they can't move the tutoring to their own facilities because many of the tutees are gang members and are afraid to ride the bus across town, through other gangs' turfs. I can't even begin to imagine what these guys are going to be like. I talked to my mom on the phone and she's convinced I'm going to get caught in a drive-by shooting or something.

Fears like this are real. As a tutor, you may have to drive, take the bus, or walk through an area where you feel less than perfectly safe. You may even be dealing with students who make you a little uneasy. Always make sure that you are comfortable with issues of safety. And then try to act as normally as possible. A terrified tutor will not be able to inspire a lot of confidence in a student.

Fear for one's personal safety is not the only thing about a site that can frighten a tutor. Sometimes social differences are just as scary. Faced with glaring differences between themselves and their tutees, some tutors even question their motives, as did this tutor who had elected to tutor in a program designed to serve gay and lesbian students. As the time to tutor approached, she became more and more nervous: "At this point, I was slightly overwhelmed. Would I not fit in because I am not gay and am involved in a heterosexual relationship? Would I not be able to relate as well as my classmate, someone who obviously understands and can empathize with the students at this center more than I? Did I choose to tutor here for the wrong reasons?"

Such feelings are not only valid but important to acknowledge. It's hard to enter a situation in which you know that you will be surrounded by people who are different from you—and to face under such conditions the daunting tasks of forming a relationship and helping someone can throw your confidence. But facing up to your doubts and working to prevent them from interfering with the relationship that you are forming with your students is one of the major challenges of tutoring.

Even tutors who have ethnicity in common with their future tutees can feel presite insecurities, as did this Latina tutor: "I'm scared to death of being rejected by the children. I'm concerned about the cultural barriers; although I am Mexican, I don't look it. I fear I might be considered a 'Pocha' or a person who denies their heritage. I know this to be a very sensitive issue."

The important thing to remember is that tutoring is a positive thing. No matter why you actually decided to tutor or take a class that involved tutoring, you are setting out to help someone and to form a fulfilling and positive relationship. If you are sincere in your efforts to relate to people and to help, they should be able to sense it and will probably respond positively. Try not to question yourself too much; instead remind yourself that tutoring can be an enjoyable experience for everyone involved.

Evaluating First Impressions

We like to think of ourselves as open-minded, yet one of the most common problems tutors face in forming relationships with their tutees is feeling too different from their students to understand them. Sometimes the differences are apparent from the first tutoring session, as they were to this white tutor.

I really wasn't very happy with the school I chose to tutor at, and I was even less happy when I arrived at the school. I thought, Is this some kind of joke? I wondered as I stood outside the dilapidated school, Am I even safe here? The neighborhood certainly didn't look very rich or even middle class. I noticed the chain-link fences running around the length of the school and images of drug dealers and kidnappers came to mind. I saw their images talking to kids through the fence trying to entice them off school grounds. . . .

I expected to be teaching highly motivated white students that were not just college bound but Harvard bound. I never even considered teaching students that were minorities who might not even be interested in learning. . . . I had to ask myself, What the hell am I doing here?

Although this tutor's response is extreme and obviously not the most desirable for a tutoring situation, it captures the thoughts that many express when they begin tutoring. Although most tutors have only the best of intentions when they go to their site, they often develop conflicting feelings and doubt that they will be able to help students who are very different from them.

Sometimes as a tutor you will be faced with prejudices you didn't even realize you had, even ones you dislike and don't want to have but that taint your impressions and behavior anyway. Upon meeting a tutee very obviously different from themselves, many tutors feel immediately uncomfortable. A tutee of a different race, gender, or even standard of appearance can exacerbate feelings of insecurity or inadequacy about a tutoring situation. At first glance, the Latina tutor's Latina tutee in the next scenario did not look like a child that she would want to befriend, and she found it difficult to want to work with her.

The moment I saw Michelle I knew that I did not want to tutor her. Prejudging her by her unkempt appearance, I doubted that we would have a cool tutoring session together. Perhaps I placed high expectations on her by hoping she would welcome me with a smile, show me her completed homework, and teach me things she likes [as her first tutee had done]. I had expected her to be a "model tutee" like Adria. Nonetheless, I took the challenge and began tutoring her.

My first impressions of Michelle were disastrous because I could not help but compare her to Adria (they were so similar and yet so different!). She was eight and was in the third grade. She had long black hair that was pulled back but hung out of her ponytail and her bangs were so long that they covered over 50 percent of her dark brown eyes. Her skin was much darker than mine, and though she was Latina too, she looked almost black. She was short and her tummy was so chubby that some of it hung out of her pink shirt. What struck me most about Michelle's unkempt appearance was her filthy hands, which, after noticing my staring, she cleaned on the pockets of her sky-blue skirt.

This example underlines the necessity of leaving expectations at the door. All tutees are different, and tutors must work to accept them unconditionally.

Adjusting to Organizational Set-Ups

On some occasions the organizational structure of the tutoring environment can point up race and gender differences. This can create an awkward situation for a tutor, particularly one who is already feeling out of place. In the next case, the man who organized the tutoring programs seemed to favor male tutors for many students, which left this female tutor feeling somewhat discriminated against.

"Could you tutor Roberto?" the director asked Daniel, not even acknowledging me.

I felt a little offended that the director asked Daniel instead of me to tutor Roberto. I remembered the progress that Roberto and I had made last week and believed that the director had asked Daniel because he was male. If a male tutor could better help Roberto, then I supported the director's decision completely. Otherwise, I felt truly discriminated against.

In other cases, the tutoring environment is oriented around a particuar race or language, one the tutor might not be familiar with. For instance, this Latina tutor found herself surrounded by African American faces at her tutoring site. When she entered her assigned classroom, the emphasis on the race of the children made her feel somewhat alien: "The first floor where the office is located is covered by posters of famous African Americans. . . . The [classroom] library is composed of an array of books dealing with African Americans. The books are mostly biographies such as Malcom X, Martin Luther King, Jr., Aretha Franklin, and Jackie Robinson."

This tutor thought it was great that the classroom teacher worked so hard to give his students positive African American role models, but she and her friend couldn't help commenting, "There don't seem to be any Latinos."

Other tutors have found themselves in alien territory when trying to tutor a child in a bilingual school that assigns homework in a language the tutor can't read. A number of our tutors were troubled at having to go back and forth between their student and other tutors who could translate the instructions on the tutee's homework before they could get down to work.

In instances like these, some degree of discomfort will exist at the beginning of the tutoring process. As a tutor, it's important not to let your discomfort get in the way of the relationship that you form with your tutee. Organizational problems don't mean that you should change sites or classrooms. Most of these difficulties fade into the background as you begin to work with your tutee. Some of them can even enrich the relationship.

Riding the Roller-Coaster Relationship

Like any relationship, tutoring involves ups and downs—periods of great confusion and of great intimacy. In a tutoring relationship with someone very different from you, you will likely experience a roller-coaster ride with more dips and turns than you experience in your everyday relationships and interactions. When you and your students have different worlds and different perceptions, you may not always see eye-to-eye or understand everything about one another. If you're prepared for these differences, you're less likely to get discouraged when even an established relationship shows signs of strain. These relationships take a lot of effort to maintain and coax into growing to their full potential.

In some cases, a *student's attitude* toward you will be the factor that makes you aware of how different you are. Some tutors are hurt when a student is cold with them and exuberant with another tutor, perhaps one of the same sex or race. Other times students are disdainful of you for having more privileges than they do and will be less than receptive to your help.

More obvious instances of difference will appear when *you put your foot in your mouth* with a student. Because many of your assumptions will differ from those of your students, it is conceivable that at least once you will say something that seems completely "wrong" and will feel bad as a consequence. Such faux pas are not only natural but to be expected in pairings such as these.

You may also have *students come to you with problems or situations you have no idea how to deal with.* Tutors raised in suburban middle-class families can be appalled at the gang activities of their inner-city students. Other tutors find themselves at odds when students approach them with a family problem that seems greater than the tutor could have withstood at the tutee's age.

In spite of the reality of these issues, and the need for taking them into consideration as you interact with your tutees, many tutors overcome them. No matter how badly you stick you foot in your mouth, or how naïve you seem to tutees, they will still know if you genuinely care about them and are trying to understand.

Allowing for the Student's Attitude

Not all tutoring pairs are matches made in heaven, and not every tutee will greet you with open arms. Just as the tutees differ from you, you may not be what they were expecting either, and it may take some time to earn their trust and establish mutual respect.

Even in minimally awkward situations, something as simple as gender difference can make a tutoring situation uncomfortable. The student's objection may not be overt, as in the first of the two cases that follow, but in both instances the tutors felt that gender differences were hampering their ability to form relationships with their students.

> "Hi Brad," I greeted him cheerfully. He looked up silent and expressionless. This always bothers me. Although I do try fervently, I don't understand why he consistently acts indifferent towards me. I have been friendly, helpful, and supportive. I always attempt to decipher the reasons behind this indifference and I conclude that it may be attributed to the fact that I'm a girl. He's at the stage where girls are viewed as "yucky."

The second tutor's student was less subtle.

> He tries to delay doing his homework. He asks whether the playground is open and when I explain that I don't know he runs off to go ask the director. I follow him, and he actually asks her if he is going to have another tutor. She says no, and he returns with me to the table. This makes me wonder if he asks this

because he had decided that he doesn't like me or whether he sees that his brother has a male tutor and feels he would be more comfortable if he had a male tutor as well.

It's important to recognize that these types of feelings, by the tutee or the tutor, are not only all right but normal.

Because tutor-tutee pairs are usually assigned, tutors can't know or choose their students in advance, and some matches are not perfect. But a slight mismatch doesn't have to be a disaster. Sometimes all it takes is a deep breath and an attempt to find something in common with the tutee. As a tutor, there is no reason you can't develop a strong relationship with a child who comes from a completely different background than yours. Tutors often find that all they need to do to build a friendship is develop some flexibility and understanding.

Putting Your Foot in Your Mouth

Even if your students aren't bothered by the differences between you, you may embarrass either yourself or your student because you are unfamiliar with how their lives differ from yours. As the tutor in the next instance found out, seemingly innocent comments can create a moment of awkwardness with a tutee:

I unknowingly put a huge foot in my mouth midway through our conversation. Kindra [her adult tutee] works in a restaurant in Westwood. Surprised by the long commute she makes from Hollywood to her job, I exclaimed, "You drive all the way to Westwood everyday?"

Her reply shocked me into a reality I had not even considered. "Honey, I don't have a car. I take the bus!" How ridiculous and ashamed I felt to assume she would drive, and how quickly she picked up on my assumption that she had a car.

Although this tutor felt vaguely uncomfortable every time she drove up to the center in her Toyota Celica, it was a moment of discomfort that passed relatively quickly and did no harm to the relationship. Similarly, in the following case, a white female tutor made a slip-up in her assumptions about her sixteen-year-old Latina student.

I was trying to explain the meaning of a "dormant" seed to Jill, when I made a big mistake. I said, "I can figure it out by knowing Spanish from high school. What do you think the root of dormant is?" I waited expectantly for the answer "*dormir*"—to sleep—but it never came.

"I don't speak Spanish," Jill said with a smile.

"You don't?" I asked. I remembered her telling me that she was celebrating Mother's Day on the tenth instead of the twelfth, because the tenth was Mexican Mother's Day. I remembered seeing her aunt come to pick her up and speaking Spanish with an adult who worked at the center. But, come to think of it, I had never actually heard Jill speak Spanish.

"I'm sorry," I apologized. "I just assumed . . ." I stopped, feeling bad. If there's one thing I've learned from my class, Sociology of Education, it is that you can't generalize one person's experience to another's. You can't stereotype, because everyone is different, and you shouldn't assume anything about anyone.

"Oh, that's okay," Jill laughed it off. "Everyone does that." She didn't seem to take offense, but I still felt guilty for making an assumption at all. Noting my confused expression, Jill explained, "My dad is Mexican and my mom is white. My parents split up when I was two, and I lived with my mom for most of my life, so I never learned Spanish. I started Spanish 1 before I moved here to my aunt's house, but I felt behind when I got here. I guess I'll take Spanish 1 next year."

I touched her arm. "I feel bad. I hope you weren't offended that I assumed you knew the language."

She brushed it off with a grin, "All my friends are fluent in Spanish, and sometimes they even forget. They'll say something to me in Spanish, and I'll just stand there staring at them. I won't say anything, and then they'll realize and translate for me, into English."

As in these examples, most small slips can probably be either ignored or laughed about. But even with the understanding that you and your tutee come from different worlds, it's important to be sensitive to issues and differences.

Coping with Situations You Have No Idea How to Deal With

When university students tutor underprivileged or at-risk students, there is often a telling socioeconomic and education gap between tutor and tutee. Sometimes the differences are apparent the moment tutors enter the neighborhood in which they will be working, and sometimes fear can get in the way of successful relationships.

What was even more striking was the physical location of the Eagles Center. I admit that the first time I stepped out of my car onto the street and walked to the building, I felt slightly nervous. As I approached the front door, I smelled the stench of urine and garbage. There were homeless men and women, barred-up shops, and dirty street gutters. . . .

As I entered the classroom one day, Billy and Matt were engaged in an intense conversation regarding the outside surroundings. As I listened to the conversation I realized that they were talking about prostitutes picking up the two boys as they leave school sometimes.

Beyond the obvious surface-level differences, tutors sometimes have to deal with more difficult issues when tutoring students of very different backgrounds. As you establish a friendship with your tutee, you will probably deal with some of your students' personal problems as well. Everyone has bad days, and, as a friend and a tutor, you will find it nearly impossible to sit down next to a sad or sullen student and settle right into math homework. As a friend, you will ask what's wrong, and as a role model, you will try to help.

Sometimes, when the students talk about their lives, they may reveal situations that seem unfair, painful, or difficult to you. You may not know what to say, and you may not know what your responsibilities are in trying to help them. For instance, the tutor in the next scenario was extremely troubled by the gang activity at his tutee's school.

> The first day of tutoring, Gabriela and Bonita witness a stabbing at their high school and the police questioned Gabriela because she dropped her backpack at the scene of the crime. The police would not give Gabriela her belongings until she admitted who committed the stabbing. Gabriela fears for her safety because everyone saw her talking to the cops and if she names the guilty people, they will come after her. When Gabriela told me what happened, she looked as though she would break down and cry. I reassured her to let all her feelings out and not to hold them inside.

The tutor was able to comfort Gabriela somewhat in the immediate aftermath, but he remained troubled that there was nothing he could do to protect her in the future.

In the next case, the tutor was shocked and scared about a gang problem that was troubling his student. The tutor and tutee had formed a fairly close relationship. The tutor had been serving as a mentor to the tutee and had been able to help him raise his grades and start thinking about the possibility of one day going to college and becoming a UCLA Bruin—if he continued to work hard in school. They considered themselves friends. One day, the tutee came in upset over a situation that the tutor had no idea how to deal with. As the tutee explained to his tutor:

> I'm telling you, there's nothing you can do. I was hanging out shooting some hoops with a couple of my friends at lunch, when these gang bangers came up to us and asked us to play three-on-three. Before I could object, my friend Dan agreed to play, and there was no way out of it.
>
> Everything was fine until the game was almost over. We were winning ten to seven, and the game was to eleven. This guy guarding me, I won't tell you his name, said that if he lost, he was going to kick my ass. Even though I did not want to lose and probably wouldn't have listened to him, I had no control over who won. Dan stole the ball from another guy and went in for a layup. Just like that, the game was over. Now this guy wants to kick my ass. Can you believe it?

For a tutor who has no experience with gang-related activities, a situation like this may not only prove overwhelming but leave the tutor feeling helpless. All the rational solutions a tutor might offer take on a different twist in the world that some of the tutees live in. Sometimes the best thing tutors can do is be good listeners and counsel as wisely as they can. In some situations, you, as a tutor, may want to get advice from someone who knows more about those kinds of problems.

One piece of advice to tutors is not to register too much shock when a student reveals these problems. Students often perceive their own situations as normal, and outrage might be inappropriate and alienate more than comfort the student.

Even if tutors find a problem shocking, they may be able to help counter it. In the following instance, the tutor's young student confided in her that he shoplifted regularly: "In the middle of a spelling lesson, Nathan changes the subject. 'Do you know how easy it is to steal from the 99 Cent store?'

"I ask him, 'How do you know you won't get caught?'

"He responded, 'They don't have cameras or nothing in there. I won't get caught.'"

This tutor was unsure how to handle the situation at the time. But she did a good job in holding her tongue, getting the full story, and not scolding the tutee on the spot. Sometimes it is better not to get involved right away; sometimes a student is testing the waters to see how a tutor will react, and the beginning of a relationship is not always the best time to try to influence a child.

Over time the tutor realized that Nathan was starved for attention, perhaps even wanting to get caught so that his parents would talk to him. He also tended to act out in class to get people to notice him.

> His mother frequently travels to Mexico and leaves Nathan with his stepfather, because his biological father is not part of his life. The catch is that the stepfather works from 3 P.M. to 1 A.M. during the week, so who takes care of Nathan? Who cooks dinner for him, helps him with his schoolwork or even puts him to bed?
>
> No wonder he's stealing from the 99 Cent store and not completing his homework. He had no direction after school. I wouldn't be surprised if he wanted to get caught shoplifting, so his parents would notice him and pay some sort of attention to him, even if it's negative.

Even if the tutor could do nothing specific to improve Nathan's home life, she had a chance to do three things: she could

encourage him not to steal, push him in the direction of some positive ways to get attention, and give him some one-on-one attention that might lessen his need to get into trouble. Nathans's major problem seems to be a lack of attention from his parents, but
for a few hours a day, he has a tutor all to himself. Do not under-
estimate the difference that a little personal attention in the form
of good tutoring can have on a child.

Overcoming Differences

Despite all the differences and difficulties in these examples, adopting the basic tutoring attitudes outlined earlier in this book can
help overcome differences between tutor and tutees. Tutoring often
succeeds between two people who seem to have little in common.

As you tutor, solutions will have to come from you, your tutee,
and the unique relationship that you have formed, as they do in the
episodes that follow. For one thing, try to minimize the difference
between yourself and your tutee—or at least maximize your "same-
ness." You are both people. Find out what you have in common and
start from there. Even people from vastly different backgrounds can
have similar interests or values. By the same token, don't stick out
more than you have to, either in dress, speech, or conversation topics. An inner-city sixteen year old probably won't have a brand new
car in the driveway on his birthday—so you don't have to mention
the one you got.

Even differences that will not go away in the time that you tutor your student need not be impenetrable barriers to your relationship. Following the premise of unconditional acceptance and
your acceptance of your students for whomever they are, your best
solution may be simply to maximize your acceptance of the differences. To accept them means to work with them and talk about
them but still to realize and be confident that dissimilar people can
create a strong and productive relationship.

The attitude of dealing with your student as an equal also comes into play when tutoring students very different from yourself. You may not always feel that you can comprehend the lives, problems, and joys of these students, but you can empathize and try to understand. The life situations of your students may seem alien to you, but get your tutees talking and take the opportunity to *let them teach you something;* with your new information, try to understand them and place yourself in their shoes. You can't necessarily solve their problems, but an open environment in which to discuss them is a gift that you *can* give.

One of the positive aspects of these differences is that they *open up avenues for conversations.* The dialogue that can spring from differences in knowledge, expectations, ambitions, and assumptions can teach both of you something about another world and a person unlike yourselves. Get your students to explain their worlds to you, but don't hesitate to explain yours to them. Show them an alternative to their world (not necessarily the best one for everyone), and a glimpse of what else is out there. And try to see and understand their lives and environments. One of the best possible consequences of putting your foot in your mouth or encountering a hostile student is the opportunity such situations create for an open, honest conversation.

Fitting in and Being as "Same" as Possible

Getting past the differences between tutors and tutees is part of the process of building a relationship. Most tutors are surprised at how much they have in common with their students. One of the first steps in the tutoring experience is finding these commonalities, and many tutors also find it effective to minimize obvious differences right off the bat.

Being "the same" is often impossible, but there are some things that you can do to fit in more, or at least not stick out in your tutoring environment, as this next tutor found.

I was tutoring at a private school, under contract with the Los Angeles Unified School District, to serve district students who are labeled as "emotionally disturbed." The "emotionally disturbed" label made me very nervous. I did not know what I was getting into. I decided to suit up; perhaps if I looked professional, the kids would take me seriously. . . .

The students standing out front when I approached the school were older than I expected. The students were ethnically integrated, wearing baggy jeans and T-shirts. Nervously, I walked past them en route to the office. In the office, I was greeted by Jim. He was wearing corduroy jeans and a tie-dyed shirt. When I saw him I wished I had worn my jeans.

When you enter a tutoring situation, it's vital to be yourself, but it may also help to be as neutral as possible. Don't attract attention to yourself or your different culture or socioeconomic background. If the students you work with come from a culture in which modesty is valued and you walk in wearing a miniskirt or jeans with holes all over them, an effective relationship will be harder to build. Tutors enter the environment of their students as guests, and the hosts' values and morals deserve respect.

The following tutor found that the same rule applied when she was working with kids from a poorer background than her own: "I noticed that they immediately spotted my jewelry and every child I helped kept staring at it. I hadn't thought that maybe I should have taken it off so I would fit in better. The reason I say 'fit in' is because it is obvious that the students at this particular school are from working-class families. At the first chance I got, I took off my rings and necklace."

This tutor felt that the signs of her class status were too blatant and might interfere with her ability to relate to the students. It was easy for her to remove her jewelry and feel more like she was on their level. Removing the jewelry also allowed the tutees to focus on tutoring rather than this sign of differentness.

Maximizing Acceptance of Your Difference

Tutors can't remove their accent, or their education, or their skin color. They may simply differ from the students they're tutoring. That's okay. In fact, it can be very valuable for tutees to develop a relationship with someone different from them and from the people they ordinarily interact with. Just as you as a tutor will learn to relate to students who are different from you, they will learn to relate to you—if you show them that you want them to.

Some tutors fear that it's impossible for them to relate to students who are very different, but that does not seem to be the case. Not only do many successful tutoring relationships grow between educated, upper- or upper-middle-class tutors and inner-city or poor youths, a flourishing private tutoring industry also faces the class difference problem, though in reverse.

Private tutors who tutor in the homes of students much more privileged than themselves often report the same discomfort as tutors who work with students much poorer than themselves, as in this example: "I had to be led out of the house because it was so big I didn't think that I was going to be able to find my way out on my own. There were three cooks in the kitchen preparing dinner. I asked Aria if her parents were having a party that night and she said no, that her parents were in London. Three cooks to make dinner for two little girls! There was also a butler and two maids that I saw in the two hours I was there. I felt like the seventh servant in the house."

Private tutors get paid well to form strong and effective tutoring relationships, even though it's obvious that few private tutors live in multimillion-dollar houses staffed with hired help. In the same way, a middle-class or even an upper-class tutor can form a relationship—often a very positive one—with a child from a working- or lower-class background.

Some tutors, such as the one who removed her jewelry, find it helpful to hide the obvious signs of their socioeconomic difference, but this isn't the only way, or even the best way, to deal with the differences. The tutees know you are different. You may come from a university, in which case they probably assume that you come from a different background. In some cases, sharing personal information can break down boundaries rather than create them.

> As I was about to take the children back to the classroom, they notice my new red 1995 Ford Mustang parked outside the school. I try to park it in a spot where no students can see my car, because I feel it's too flashy. I just feel awkward because I don't want the children to think of me as just some rich college kid. I also didn't want it to be the topic of my conversations with the students. I want to help tutor them, not discuss cars.
> Anyway, the lunch table where I gave them their spelling list was in direct view of my Mustang, and Daniel said, "Check out that new Mustang! I think Mr. Mooney drives one of those."
> Erin jumped in, "No, Mr. Mooney's is different. Is that yours, Miss Karen?"
> I was on the spot, and I had to respond so I told them, "No, it's not." I feel so guilty about lying to them. Instead I should have trusted the fact that they would have enjoyed knowing what kind of car I drove, as they did about Mr. Mooney's car.

Opening up a Conversation

In other scenarios, tutors' coming from a different background than their tutees' can benefit the students. As such a tutor, you have the opportunity to expose tutees to ideas and ambitions that they may never have had contact with. Just as working with and forming a relationship with a person quite different from yourself is interesting and eye-opening, tutees may have the same experience with you. You are foreign to their world, but that doesn't mean that they can't learn something from you.

You have a wealth of information that many students have never been exposed to, especially concerning academic success. You also have resources that they do not have access to. For instance, tutors are often able to give their students valuable information about preparing for college. Sometimes the tutor is the only resource a tutee has for this kind of information. Other times it is simply more effective coming from someone who is more of a peer and a friend than an authority figure.

When you deal with students from a very different background than yours, you will often find yourself cast in the role of "the other." You may be foreign to their neighborhoods, even feared there. You may represent employers that they dislike or privileged people who oppress them. Just as you will be forced to confront your stereotypes when you tutor students unlike yourself, they will be forced to confront theirs.

This clash of expectations can cause tension in the relationship, which some tutors like to take head on, often to the benefit of both parties. In the next scenario, the tutor places himself in a "rich white" category by his familiarity with a posh Beverly Hills restaurant that has donated some bread to the tutoring center. When his tutee reacts negatively, the tutor uses the opportunity presented for a candid conversation on race and privilege.

On the table were several packages of bread from a restaurant called Il Fornaio. I told him, "That restaurant is in Beverly Hills."

He immediately squished his face together, wrinkling his nose, and said, "I hate Beverly Hills." When I asked him why, he made a disturbing comment that "rich people are uptight and rude."

I asked, "Do you think Magic Johnson, who is obviously rich, is rude?"

He responded with an even worse comment, saying, "It is

just white people who are rude." I then asked, "Do you think Mike Piazza, the star of the Dodgers who is also rich, is rude?"

He said, "No."

And I explained, "Mike is an example of why you might not want to form opinions about people before you meet them. I understand that historically, white rich men have brought about the inequalities in society by controlling government, but I want you to know that if you want to be treated equally, you should treat others equally as well. Having a predetermined opinion about an individual based on his or her skin color, or income, is not right."

He said, "I guess I never thought about it that way. It's just that most of the rich white people I see, like at the television studios [he goes with his youth group], don't even say hi to me. I'm sorry, I know I shouldn't stereotype." Since he understood, we ended the conversation.

For the most part, tutors find that differences which at first glance seem impossible to work with are not that overwhelming. There's no reason why a tutoring relationship has to be homogeneous. What's more, tutors often find that "very different" students have a lot to teach *them*, once the lines of communication are open. Like the following white male tutor, many tutors have enjoyed learning new words in the student's native tongue as they work to increase their tutee's English proficiency.

The supervisor asks me if I want to teach English. This tutee speaks minimal English. And, even worse, I do not speak Spanish. Of course, though, I am up to the challenge. I go and get flashcards from the rolling bin. I show him the picture, he reads the word. I then correct his pronunciation if it needs correcting. After a few words I realize it's going well.

I try to explain to him that he can teach me Spanish while I teach him English. He doesn't understand. Another tutor who speaks Spanish relays my message to Julio. He likes that idea. I get out a piece of paper and a pen and for every word that we do, I say [the English], then he says [the English]. Then he says the Spanish equivalent, then I say the Spanish equivalent. Then I have him write down the English word next to the Spanish word. He likes this form of learning and I think it is working well.

After doing about forty words or so, I turn to sentence use. I start with "I am a" and things like that. He catches on fast and before we know it we are making sentences about me and him. "I am a man." "You are a man." "I am tall." "You are small."

Many tutors who pick up some Spanish or another language from their students are then able to put their new skills to use on other limited-English-speaking tutees.

Beyond languages, tutors also learn a great deal about other religions and cultures by talking to their students about after-school activities and holiday celebrations. Even from students whose differentness may look rather unsavory at the beginning, there is much to be learned. The tutor who worked with paroled gang found that discussions with her students gave her a broader view of her city and the "other" people who lived there.

I was fascinated as Oscar described to me how the various gangs are broken into subgroups and cliques and what the tags that we see all over the city stand for. That the hierarchy is so intricate and complex was shocking to me. It was not what I had expected from groups of "thugs." . . . In talking to him I could see just how pervasive this way of life was to him, that he had grown up in a gang and that it was very much of what he knew.

As he explained to me how he could attack someone just for being in another gang, the reasons, completely absurd to me before, became somewhat clearer. Although I can't say that I approve of gang life, I feel like I have a better understanding of what was just a cartoon picture to me before. I also better understand that the boys in them are just that: boys. They aren't monsters. We had the kids fill out a form in which they had to write a bit about themselves. One of the questions was, "Who do you admire most?" From this group of convicted delinquents, one answer was unanimous. Their moms. How can we say these kids are not saveable?

Through tutoring, this tutor gained compassion and understanding for a group of people with whom she might never otherwise have made contact. Her new knowledge will affect the way she sees others, interprets the news, and discusses topics such as crime and poverty. In the end, for all the difficulties that can arise from tutoring those who are different, the benefits are generally greater, for all parties involved.

Recommended Reading

We have made little effort to document the ways in which race, ethnicity, gender, social class, religion, and sexual orientation are ignored in traditional education. This institutional neglect has deeply divided poor students and students of color from their teachers and has occurred to the intellectual detriment of students, their teachers, and society.

One classic book that documents the devastating treatment of poor children and the resistance by middle- and upper-class parents to improving poor schools in their own communities is Jonathan Kozol's *Savage Inequalities* (1991). Kozol began his critique of U.S. public education in 1967 with a savage indictment of the educational system's response to poor black children in Boston. In *Death at an Early Age* (1968), he describes conditions so horrific that one wonders how Americans, teachers, and administrators can endure their own brutality and insensitivity to these children. In *Savage Inequalities* he shows not only how these conditions still exist in the 1990s, but that they occur throughout the United States.

In spite of (or perhaps, in part, because of) the problems so poignantly depicted by Kozol, some educators are addressing the neglect of students' background variables that we have described in this chapter. They document that a focus on various and personal cultures is useful and valuable for students. Mike Rose, in *Possible Lives* (1995), travels America and finds teachers in different cities and locales building class curriculums geared to the cultural backgrounds of their students.

Sonia Nieto in *Affirming Diversity* (1996) shows how race, religion, immigrant status, gender, and ethnicity are very significant factors in students' motivation to learn and to become educated.

Similarly, Lisa Delpit's *Other People's Children* (1995) is a collection of essays that describes the special care that must be taken when teaching children from diverse race and class backgrounds. For instance, she explicates some of the cultural differences in the ways African American and white parents direct and discipline their children and the repercussions of these differences on classroom management. Like Rose and Nieto, she discusses ways to preserve children's diverse cultural knowledge and pride, but she also emphasizes the importance of teaching disadvantaged students the ways of the dominant culture they will need to survive and succeed in the United States.

For a more detailed look at the verbal and cultural differences often found between teachers and students, see Shirley Heath's *Ways with Words* (1983) or "Questioning at Home and at School: A Comparative Study" (1982). In these pieces, educator, linguist, and anthropologist Shirley Brice Heath shares a number of provocative insights into the cultural-linguistic differences between working-class black children and their often white middle-class teachers. By comparing the verbal questions and cues black families and educators use to those used by white parents and teachers, Heath shows dramatically how subtly incongruent these styles can be, and how easily a white teacher might label a black child uncooperative or unmanageable, when the real problem is that student and teacher are not understanding one another.

5
Other Adults: Parents, Teachers, and Administrators

The tutor, the tutee, and their mutual trust shape every tutoring relationship. As a tutor, you and your tutee will work together to create the foundation for a successful tutoring partnership. Throughout tutoring, however, the many other adults who are integral parts of your tutees' lives will influence them in many ways—their parents and the teachers and administrators of their schools and tutoring sites.

Their greatest impact comes from their attitudes toward the tutee. For instance, believing in students can give them the support and confidence that enable them to perform up to their potential, and labeling them as "slow" or neglecting them can be devastating for their emotional health and development. Tutees can take these attitudes on themselves, in which case they may impede your tutees' progress and undermine their belief in their abilities and potential. Just as other adults' positive attitudes and support may enhance your interaction with your tutee, their negative influence can impede your relationship and your tutee's academic and social progress.

A tutor's awareness and sensitivity to the presence and influence of these significant other adults are therefore not just necessary, but vital. When the involvement of other adults serves the best interest of tutees, tutors should welcome it. However, as a tutor, you will often encounter situations involving other adults that jeopardize the mental, emotional, and sometimes the physical health of your tutee. You need to be able to recognize and negotiate the effects these influential adults have.

Parents and teachers have a huge amount of influence in shaping the environments in which your students spend most of their time. Often these influences are positive and flow from a supportive *attitude*. Parents and teachers can work wonders with students when they act as encouraging and enthusiastic leaders and role models. The students' resulting confidence makes your job as a tutor considerably easier.

The more parent and teacher *involvement* you see in the lives of your students, the more positive their learning environment is likely to be. Involved parents go out of their way to know what's going on and get advantages for their children. Involved and attentive teachers stay on top of what you are working on with your students, monitor their progress, and make sure that the work they give you continues to be challenging.

Another obvious way that the adults in your tutee's life can help make your job easier is by assigning *challenging and interesting tasks*. Teachers who assign exciting homework and provide a dynamic curriculum produce kids willing to sit down with their tutor and do their work.

On the flip side, other adults in your students' lives may have a negative impact. A tutor must always be alert to such influences, for even though they in no way make the tutoring relationship impossible, they erect obstacles. And before tutors can actively work to hurdle these, they have to recognize them.

One of the most common negative attitudes that students face, from both parents and teachers, shows up in a *lack of involvement*. Because there are many possible reasons for adults, particularly parents, to remain uninvolved in their kids' education, we suggest that tutors spend some time observing and trying to understand all the circumstances before deciding that a parent or set of parents is *neglectful.* Some parents don't get involved because they are too busy, they lack the education or language skills to help their children, or they have a different class orientation to school than you do. It would be wise for the tutor to work under the assumption that all parents want their children to succeed, even if they do not know how to go about helping them do it. Regardless, children lacking guidance and attention can greatly benefit from the couple of hours a week that they spend with a tutor.

Another form of neglect that makes a tutor's job harder occurs when teachers assign students *boring, rote exercises* and provide little motivation to do them. When teachers assign work that does nothing to inspire your students, it is up to you, as a tutor, to inject some creativity and make their homework fun.

One of the saddest things that the adults involved with your students can do is pigeonhole them with *labels.* Unfortunately, labeling is one of the most common problems that tutors run up against. Students who have heard—often—that they are stupid or lazy are sometimes the hardest to motivate. Tutors get especially frustrated at labels when they can see no basis for them in the child. Here again, tutors must use their influence as adults in the student's life to combat the negative stereotypes.

Although tutors are the first to applaud the other adults who fill their students with positive attitudes, they also are highly disturbed by damaging negative influences they see. One of the most common questions that tutors ask themselves and each other is *"What can I do to help?"* The answer is not an easy one. In a classroom, a tutor is a guest in the teacher's domain and does not have the authority to change a teacher's curriculum or attitude toward students. Dealing directly with parents also places a tutor in a position of relative helplessness. Who are tutors to tell parents how to raise their children?

Tutors can nevertheless mediate and find solutions to some of the negative forces in the lives of tutees. Developing a close relationship with the other adults may be the wisest investment a tutor can make, aside from developing a close relationship with the tutee. Building an effective partnership with parents, teachers, and administrators will create understanding and cooperation, which will work to tutees' best interests. Establishing this effective partnership often requires the tutor's initiative, forbearance, and patience. Although some feel confident in their social skills, others may feel uncomfortable and inadequate developing these relationships. Yet these skills improve over time. Tutors who keep in mind the best interests of their tutees can always draw strength from there.

Attitudes and Involvement of the Other Adults

Involved and supportive parents and teachers can be your greatest asset as a tutor. They can give you relevant background information on your students, tell you their areas of strength and weakness and other qualities that may facilitate your tutoring experience from the start. Beyond that, parents and teachers who are *willing to work closely with tutors* often form good teams. Tutors are almost always the most effective when they have the cooperation of parents, teachers, and other adults whom the child either works with or respects.

Even if the other adults in your students' lives won't or can't work directly with you, their simple *involvement in the lives of your students* can create an good environment for tutoring. When students know that adults care about them, they are more willing to open up with other adults, including you.

Involvement with the Tutors

Many tutors find that their most successful tutoring comes out of strong partnerships with the student's parents, teachers, or both. When the adults in a child's life work together as a team they can use each other to reinforce values and keep up confidence. They can also work together to build the student up in weaknesses that may be common to home, school, and tutoring.

In the following case, the tutor found that interacting with her tutee's mother set a great foundation for their partnership in assisting the tutee. Joe's mom was able to bolster his confidence not only by praising him, but by praising him to his tutor, someone else who would be proud of his accomplishment and continue the work of encouraging him to try. In this case, the tutor and the parent were sharing the task of helping Joe with his homework, which made the partnership even more successful.

> Joe wanted to sit at the far round table and said that he had fun homework today. Louise, his mother, excitedly came over and said, "Joe, show Lisa your spelling test."
>
> I said, "Oh, great, how did it go?"
>
> She said proudly, "Every day last week, I make him sit down and work on those words." It was Joe's first spelling test. He handed it to her and took off to look around the center. She showed me how he got all but two correct, minimizing his errors by showing me how he confused the two words. She seemed very pleased.

Tutors who interact with their tutee's parents also may get a sense of how the parents feel about their child's education, and what teaching methods they would prefer. Even if in some cases this is not necessary, it helps to form a good relationship with the parents and can make tutoring sessions, particularly with young students who don't have that much official "work" more productive. The following Latina tutor found out a lot about what her six-year-old Latina tutee's family wanted her to focus on by talking with the student's mother.

> Lucia's mother and I had a small conversation on bilingual education that was triggered by my asking how much English

Lucia knows. To my questions, Delia responded that "Lucia used to know more English when she was in the Mar Vista preschool than she knows now that she's going to kindergarten." Delia showed some disappointment when she stated this.

Without further questioning, Delia volunteered her opinion on her daughter's education. She explained to me that Lucia is a smart young girl who learns new stuff pretty quickly. She said that she is convinced that if teachers at her kindergarten spoke to her in English, she would learn it rather quickly. Delia told me that the staff at Mar Vista show that they really care about student learning. She said that most of the things that Lucia knows now, such as writing her name, counting to twenty, and the vowels were taught to her in preschool. Delia feels that Lucia is not being challenged in her new school.

Before Delia left, I asked her what language she prefers that I speak to Lucia in during tutoring. "Speak to her in both," she said.

Similarly, teachers receptive to working with tutors can enrich the tutoring experiences of their students. In the following case, the tutor was empowered by the great attitude of most of the teachers with whom she would be working.

Today I mainly observed because the teachers wanted me to get a feel of the class to see what I would be comfortable with and to see what it is that they want me to do. I was very welcome in two of the classes, Mrs. Edwards's and Mrs. McCall's. They were both extremely receptive towards me, showed me around, gave me a few things to do and told me what they would be expecting of me in the future. The third teacher, Mrs. Lowry, said nothing to me from the moment I walked in the door.

A close partnership between teachers and tutors can go a long way in benefiting a student. The two adults can work together not only to figure out the needs of students and the best way to address them, but to monitor their progress and keep each other abreast of developments that might otherwise be missed—either because the teacher is busy with the other students or because the tutor is only in class a few hours a week.

The cooperation and help of teachers who have developed relationships with the children whom you are working with can help you develop your own. Teachers sometimes use their power to help tutors out, as in this incident in which a tutor was rescued by a teacher she hadn't even met yet.

> A teacher whose class was outside for recess saw how uncontrollable Gary and Phillip were being and approached the bench we were sitting on. She said to Phillip, with a thick Hispanic accent, "Phillip, what are you doing to this poor young lady? Can't you guys behave for her?" The teacher was very polite and obviously knew them both on a personal level.

Similarly, any other adults who have a relationship with a tutee, from volunteers at the tutoring site or classroom to other parents, can help when a tutor is struggling with a child. As a tutor, don't be afraid to ask for help from an adult who may have more resources or leverage than you have. As the female Jewish tutor in the next example found when working with Elsa, her stubborn seven-year-old Latina student, a little gentle persuasion from someone in power is sometimes all is takes to get a tutor some respect or cooperation.

> Once I had officially said "No" to her, she became more blatant in her defiance. "I not gonna do it," she told me coyly, with a great big smile on her face.
>
> I dealt with this by informing her, "You need to do it before we can do anything else." We went back and forth for nearly

ten minutes—she insisting that she wasn't going to do it or she couldn't do it, and me replying that she needed to do it and she could do it. I told her that I knew she was smart at math because we had worked on numbers last week. Finally, I pointed to the line that said, "*Nombre*," and prompted her to fill it in. She wrote "Elizabeth" on the line. I reminded her that her name was not "Elizabeth" it was Elsa, and that she needed to write her real name down. With a big smile on her face, she declared that Elizabeth was her real name.

There were only so many battles I could fight with her, so I decided to leave the name alone and start working on the math problems. It was agonizingly slow, because she wanted me to just write down the answers for her. She continued to be distracted, to wander off, or to color on her arms. I just kept plodding along, prompting addition by holding up my fingers to help her count.

We mostly worked in Spanish, though I speak very little. The concept of adding seemed to make more sense to her in Spanish. After what seemed to be forever, but was actually only fifteen minutes, we finished the sheet. When Anna [the site director] walked by, I used what is called an "overheard compliment." I spoke loudly enough for Elsa to hear, and informed Anna of how well Elsa had done her homework. The only problem, I said, was that she had put the wrong name at the top of the paper.

Anna glanced at the paper and told Elsa to put her name at the top. They spoke in Spanish for a few minutes, and then Anna repeated her instructions. After Elsa erased the name Elizabeth and wrote her own, Anna grinned at me, "She likes to play games."

Elsa had been coming to the center since she was a baby. She knew the rules and had a good relationship with Anna. In asking for help, the tutor was not admitting a weakness, she simply used Anna as a resource to prove to Elsa that she had some authority and that what she was asking was in fact reasonable. Some level of cooperation between teacher and tutor is essential, and the more the teachers and other adults involved with your student are willing to work with you, the easier your job will be.

General Interest and Involvement in the Students' Lives

Some parents and teachers do not have the time or the abilities to get involved in tutors' relationships with their students. Sometimes tutees' parents aren't able to help out in the classroom and be directly involved in their education in that way. But even if the other adults in students' lives cannot help directly, they affect the tutoring relationship simply in the ways that they interact with their children, and in the attitudes they impart to them.

In the next example, the parent did not have the resources to help her children very much academically. But she did everything in her power to encourage her children to get a good education and follow their dreams.

Ms. Trey drove Brent and Tanisha to UCLA every Saturday, so the kids could participate in the Saturday Outreach Program. She was a single mother, living in the projects, working hard to support her kids. Despite her limited resources, she managed to bring her children to UCLA campus. After a while, when her work schedule made it impossible for her to bring the kids to school, she started a car-pool program in the neighborhood with the help of the tutors.

I developed the deepest level of respect and admiration for her caring and intelligent ways. She motivated me to do a better job every Saturday I went out there.

This parent's involvement in her children's lives affected the tutoring both directly and indirectly. Not only did she provide this great opportunity for her children, her positive attitude worked to further motivate her kids' tutor. She accomplished this difficult task despite her limited resources, and despite her own limited educational background.

Some parents who support their children in their schoolwork and other areas of life are still not eager to form a close relationship with their tutor. Sometimes they are also leery of their child and a tutor forming too close a relationship. Generally, we emphasize being friendly and trying to arrange some kind of outing for your tutee, but this can make some parents uncomfortable. In the following case, a tutor who had formed a really close relationship with his student had planned to take him to visit the UCLA campus, the student's dream school. Both tutor and student were excited, but when the tutor called his student's parents to ask permission, they postponed and discouraged the trip.

> I stopped talking to wait for her response. I felt that I made a pretty good point, but I did not feel that great about the situation. After all, if I had a twelve-year-old son, I would be scared to let him go off with somebody I had never met, even if it was his tutor. My feeling was pretty much right on.
>
> "Well, Jack, I think that a tour of UCLA would be something that Ben would really like to do. He has been talking about it to me all the time. It is just that I am not sure if it would work out. Ben is very busy with schoolwork and his final exams are coming up. Also, as soon as he finishes school, he will be going to work for his father. Why don't I discuss it with Mr. Martinez, and then we can discuss it again at the party on Wednesday."

In these cases, of course, the parents win. But, as a tutor, try to be open to your students and offer the hand of friendship nevertheless, even if they cannot always take it. Be understanding about the parents' caution. Although it is wonderful when parents and students can work together, it is not always possible and should not affect your relationship with the student.

Discouragement and Lack of Involvement

In the same way that involvement and encouragement can boost a student's confidence and achievement, neglect and lack of understanding can devastate anyone's child's self-esteem and motivation. Tutors sometimes feel that both teachers and parents are guilty of apathy where their tutee is concerned, a very frustrating situation.

The child in the next example had been hospitalized for about two years because of leukemia, during which he socialized only with adults and his family and received a lot of attention. As a result he was unskilled in socializing with children his own age and, in addition, outside of his health problems apparently got very little care at home. Because he was not able to socialize at school and had little support from his parents, Justin started turning to his tutor for help. One afternoon he called to ask his tutor to help him with his homework. The tutor learned that he was home alone with a housekeeper who spoke only Spanish. "I do not know how they communicate, but obviously Justin needs attention at home. Unfortunately, he needs this attention from the two people who seems to be too caught up in themselves right now. Hopefully both parents will realize his needs before it is too late."

Apathy from teachers can be just as difficult for tutors to deal with. When students realize that teachers don't care, they don't care either. Students whose teachers are too uninvolved to expect quality work will live up to that low expectation and do as little as possible. The following tutor, a Latina, did not know what to do about the dishonest attitude that the teacher's uncaring behavior had fostered in her tutee. Her student, a fifteen-year-old African American female, found little incentive not to cheat.

After a brief introduction, Summer and I began working on her Spanish homework. "I have a test tomorrow and I need to know everything in Chapter 7 before the test," she said as she handed me her Spanish book. I began to tutor her by asking her what she knew in Chapter 7 and she said, "*Nada,*" and stared at me, looking for answers. When I opened the book to Chapter 7, I asked her to work on translating the nouns that were listed in Spanish and instead she began talking about her boyfriend and about how she skipped classes often and how she could get away with lying to her parents without being caught.

Her conversation was irrelevant and distracting to our session but I listened attentively, waiting for clues that might help me understand enough about her persona to be able to relate her to the material in her book. I reminded her that we needed to study for the exam and she assured me that studying was not necessary in her class.

She took out a sheet of paper and copied many of the nouns listed in her book and asked me what they meant in English, and I told her. Then, she proudly put that sheet of paper underneath many other blank pages and told me how easily she could fool her teacher during the test. She told me that her teacher does not monitor the exams and often reads the newspaper while everyone (including her) pulls out the page with the answers and writes them down on the test paper.

Still other adults not only seem disinterested in their students but go out of their way to be critical, even mean, which is always hard for a tutor to watch. This Asian female tutor was at a loss for words when she heard a substitute teacher criticize the fourth-grade class she was working in.

I was shocked at some of the comments that Mr. James made to the students about their drawings. To one child he said, "You made the vase too big. You better start all over on the back." He suggested to some of the other children as well that they start all over because they did it wrong. I was surprised that Mr. James felt it was all right to criticize the children's drawing rather than encourage them.

When he noticed that some of the children had barely drawn anything he said, "What's the matter, this is supposed to be fun." I felt angry that he could claim that the assignment was supposed to be fun, while at the same time he was demanding and critical.

Because of his critical remarks I could see that most of the children were critical of themselves. Most of the children were very dissatisfied with their drawings, though, in my opinion, they were fine. They would say things like "This is hard," or "I don't like mine," or "Forget it."

Although this comment from a substitute teacher probably had only a temporary effect on the children, from this example it's easy to see how fragile the egos of some young children are and how cruel comments can cause them to give up on themselves.

Even more tragic than a neglected or discouraged student are the students whose influential adults refuse to accept them for who they are. Whether they do not meet their parents' expectations, or they have had a bad experience with a teacher, it's sad to see students struggle without the help of those who should be there to support them. The devastating effect on students of their parents' ostracism is evident in the example that follows, in which the tutee had to leave home because his style of living was unacceptable to his mother. "The theme of Chris's paper is 'diversity in society,' so he focused on how the gay community treats him and his gay friends: 'I am frustrated because I believe the community looks at me like I am a "piece of meat" and a "sex toy." I want to be accepted for who I am—a hardworking, smart young male who has many important skills and abilities.'"

Chris feels ignored and worthless. His letter is addressed to his mom, who knows he is gay but does not support his choice. He felt it was important to tell her how different his life is and the troubles he faces living on his own. Although the tutor can do little to affect her student's relationship with his mother, she can give him some of the unconditional support and acceptance he so desperately needs.

Assignments and Activities

A teacher's positive involvement with the classroom can also indirectly enhance the tutor-tutee relationship by providing a conducive learning environment and making learning desirable and fun. Many tutors have found that interesting and intriguing activities involve students and incite them to work and learn. Boring classroom activities are reflected in students' reactions and behaviors—for example, students in a previous chapter got excited about reading *Romeo and Juliet* with their tutor but plodded through their social studies reading with no interest. When teacher-assigned activities are dull or rote, tutors have to work a lot harder to keep their students focused and interested.

Sometimes teachers seem to give assignments without considering student interest or time. Tutors are often frustrated with work that seems assigned to keep students busy, not to get them involved in the subject matter. The white female tutor in the following scenario was repeatedly at odds with her sixteen-year-old Latina student's biology homework.

Today she has biology homework. Remembering how her history class didn't have enough books to go around, I nervously asked if she had a biology book. I knew that I wouldn't be any help unless she had a book to which to refer. She did. For some strange reason, her teacher had assigned all the "Review It" sections of the entire chapter for one night of homework. That kept us busy.

I think that it was poor planning on the teacher's part to pack so much work in one night of homework, because we wound up just reading through the text to find the answers—not reading it for comprehension. The concepts were relatively easy—Darwin, natural selection, artificial insemination, etc. I've learned these concepts many times in science classes. With the brief review I got from reading the chapter, I was fairly confident about my comprehension.

I got the distinct impression, however, that Angela was not getting much out of the assignment. I tried to let her come up with an attempt at the answers before I helped her out, and she was often wrong. It seemed as though she was just skimming for answers or the key words used in the question. I did try to explain the main concepts in further depth, but she was mostly concerned with getting this massive assignment done before our time was up. She spent the entire hour and a half writing furiously and she still barely finished.

After seeing the types of assignments Angela is given from her teachers at school, I am disappointed. I feel that the assignments are very superficial and are mostly busywork. When the assignments *are* productive, I feel as though she has been given no knowledge in class to use in the context of the assignments. The "Review It" questions might have been a review if the teacher had presented the material to the students earlier in a method that was comprehensible to them. Angela said that they had read part of the chapter in class.

Some activities make learning not only boring but downright impossible. The white female tutor in the next example was extremely frustrated with the work that her seventh-grade Latina student brought to tutoring, and even more frustrated when she found that the problems lay in the teacher's instructions.

> After we were done with the math problems, she pulled out her torn-up dictionary that was falling apart and a vocabulary list. I looked at what was written on the sheet, and some of them were not words. I asked her, "Where did you get these?"
>
> She mumbled, "My neighbor wrote them down in class, and he is stupid." I was so confused.
>
> It took almost fifteen minutes to understand how these supposed "words" were written down in her possession. She wasn't telling me the whole story. I had to keep probing. I was getting really frustrated because she knew what happened and she was just not telling me. I finally figured out that the boy next to her copied down the word for her and she couldn't understand his handwriting so she just left it and didn't realize what she wrote down until I confronted her about it.
>
> She told me she tried to look them up and they weren't in the dictionary and she asked me why. I said, "Nancy, it is because they are *not words*." I then told her that she needs to go and talk to the teacher the next day first thing and tell her what happened. I then told her to write her own words down from the board next time. She said that her teacher tells the students to copy them from their neighbor, then exchange. I thought this was ridiculous.

Labeling

One of the most serious issues that tutors face is a process called labeling. *Labeling* means telling students something about themselves— that they are "slow," or "troublemakers," or "bad test takers."

Students tend to internalize these labels, and to compute their own worth accordingly. Negative labels almost always reduce students' confidence and self-esteem.

Labels have other effects as well. They tend to become self-fulfilling prophesies. Students labeled as "slow" have little motivation to challenge themselves, to prove themselves by doing work they have been told is too hard for them. They thus fulfill the labeler's prophecy; they become just what the label said they were. Labels also affect the way that teachers and other adults deal with children. Told that students are "slow," adults usually treat them in a certain way, sometimes not challenging them, other times patronizing them. It is for exactly this reason that labels become so salient for tutors.

Tutors are usually assigned to work with students who need extra help—the students most likely to be negatively labeled. Many tutors find themselves biased by the label, which affects their teaching and their ability to form a relationship. Other times, tutors find that the labels are wrong, that "slow" students excel when given the proper one-on-one work and encouragement.

Tutors often do not even meet the student's labeler. Many students carry labels around for years, heavy and unwanted baggage. But especially frustrating to tutors is watching the labeling process in action, watching a student they feel has potential be demoralized by someone the student loves and respects: "At 6:10 Dena's mother came for her and was surprised to see us playing with the animals. I told her we finished our homework and I had read a couple of stories and looked up words in the dictionary. I told her Dena was feeling a little bit tired and wanted a change of atmosphere. Dena's mother then said her daughter was lazy. I felt so bad for Dena when her mother said that right in front of her."

When a parent frequently expresses this kind of attitude over years of a child's life, the child inevitably internalizes it. Other tutors who worked with Dena and her mother over the course of a few years expressed the same concern as this tutor. Usually, as soon as her mother left the educational center, Dena would vent and do turn her attention away from her homework, or daydream while the tutor was attempting to assist her. On a few occasions her excuse for not paying attention was "because I am lazy." She had learned to live up to her mother's expectations.

The labels that parents attach to their children are not always as specific as "lazy," but more subtle labels can be equally damaging. Favoritism, the practice of praising or actively favoring one student or child to the detriment of another, is a common form of labeling that often doesn't seem as harmful to the people who practice it, because it involves speaking positively of at least one child. In the following example, parent comparisons of their two children became a source of insecurity for their son. During tutoring Carlos often mentioned his twin sister and how smart she is.

> She is his twin but different from Carlos. He always mentions how much smarter she is but that he is reluctant to ask her for help. He said he could do it on his own. He also mentioned how he tends to care for the house and his family more than her. Carlos's experience in his family seems to have influenced his expression of self. I feel that he feels inadequate in some aspect in his life which affects his academics. He may not have had enough attention and encouragement to believe in himself, thus putting him in the situation he is in.

Carlos's parents' contrasting expectations for him and his sister at home have significantly affected his educational progress. In this example, Carlos's parents hold a rather traditional expectation of him: to be the "man of the house" and support the family.

Favoritism also occurs fairly often in the classroom. Sometimes it happens inadvertently, as when teachers try to make examples and role models out of students who excel. Other times, teachers simply prefer some kids over others, and their favoritism can substantially affect a less preferred student's confidence and effort level.

> While tutoring, Alberto and Bert always tutor close to each other. At times, they would begin their conversations about how their school is. They always talk about their history teacher. They say he hates them. He treats them differently from the other students and always points them out. Their teacher always gets mad at them, but they do not seem to know why and do not really care either. Kelly, Bert's tutor, and I ask them if they knew, but they just shrugged their shoulders.
>
> This treatment may not matter to them, but it could affect their academic performance and their academic esteem. Alberto has shared with me some stories. One story that sticks to mind and really worries me was a story of one of his test days. Alberto had forgotten to do some parts for the exam—the teacher handed out a list of questions before the exam. "The girl in front of me didn't have her stuff either. We told the teacher but he didn't care. . . . He let her use her book, but he wouldn't let me," he recalled.
>
> "Oh, my gosh! Why do you think that he did that to you?" I asked.
>
> He replied, "He does not like me."

Students are often told by their parents to listen to their teachers and take them seriously, because "they know what is best for you." Unfortunately, taking a teacher's bias seriously can easily undermine students' confidence in their academic potential. The unhappy effect of a teacher's comment is evident in the following example.

> The substitute teacher was a man that I would never wish to be a teacher for anyone's children. "They told me that this was

supposed to be a Magnet School and that you guys are supposed to be smarter than regular students. . . . You're not smarter. . . . Maybe one or two of you are, but you guys aren't smarter."

I was looking at the students' faces when he said this and for a split second they had all been shocked by what he said and they stopped what they were doing. After a while they continued to work. But, all the kids were in such low spirits.

If a comment from a substitute, whom the students have not even had a chance to grow to like or respect, has this obvious an effect, imagine what a respected teacher might do.

Fortunately, most teachers are not this overt. Most care deeply about their students and wouldn't think of deliberately doing anything to hurt them. But, working within the system, teachers are often forced to label, and time constraints make it easy for teachers to overlook students' potential. Labeling their class or a group of students tends to make a teacher's job easier and provides a sense of order. Sometimes, a teacher will label students or put them down in order to "help" the tutor. For instance, this is how one teacher introduced a tutor to the fifth-graders she would be working with: "'These kids are way behind; they are at first- and second-grade reading levels. Just humor them, okay?' The teacher went on about how she had to find second-grade reading books for the children and how even those books were very difficult." The tutor thus started her time with her students with a handicap; she was told they weren't worth her help. The same students are bombarded daily with statements that they are not only inadequate, but not even worth working with.

In the next case, the teacher tried to help a tutor by explaining her first-grade student's problem. Even though she was somewhat kinder toward the child than the teacher in the previous example, her labels, which put down his family, were no less damaging.

She spoke about the little boy I would be working with. "There's a little boy in the first grade by the name of Manuel. He has a hard time with motor skills, hand coordination . . . and can barely use a scissors."

Here, I thought, "Okay, how'd he get to first grade?" The teacher answered my thoughts when she proceeded to say, "He never went to kindergarten . . . he comes from a family of nine children. His mom and dad are illiterate . . . it's almost as if he's neglected . . . like a baby, just out of diapers. Yet he's extremely polite and sweet, no behavior problems at all. He speaks mostly Spanish, but he can also speak English. . . . Sound like a challenge?"

I was a little stunned at the load of information she had just told me, yet I responded with, "I'd be happy to help him out."

[I met Manuel and noticed that he was shy, but he answered my questions and was willing to work.] "So, Manuel, do you want to work on numbers, letters, or shapes?" I asked.

Manuel replied, "Numbers," and pointed to the chart the teacher gave me. He spoke in a quiet low voice that seemed to match his face—inanimate and indifferent. Then he smiled randomly, "I can count to one hundred."

I responded, "Wow, that's good." For the next few minutes or so I played a game with him. I recited a number and then asked him to point to it on the chart. He did them all correctly. Then I pointed to a number and asked him to tell me what it was. Again, every response was correct, with only a few moments of hesitation for larger numbers. I thought to myself, "This boy seems to be doing okay. What's all this stuff the first teacher was telling me about?" I had to ignore my expectation from the description the first teacher gave and just go with the initial feelings I got from working with him. In other words, I felt he was smarter than she made him out to be.

Oftentimes, teachers feel that their attitude toward a student is substantiated by a specific incident that proved the student was incapable of learning certain subjects according to the teacher's standard. Teachers frequently draw these conclusions with little regard for where students come from, their family life, and whether they are ready to open up and work their best.

> Veronica looked really engrossed in her assignment. I realize that the teacher had given up on her because she had told me that Veronica could not speak English at all. Had she pushed a little harder, she would have noticed that Veronica was really scared of making a mistake. However, when you explain to someone that it is okay to mess up, all of a sudden that person will be encouraged to try with the fears and anxieties; this will then help the student learn. This lets the student know that the tutor is really paying attention to what is important to her. . . . When I first worked with Veronica, the teacher made it seem as if there was no hope for her. But I had a completely different experience with the student.

Here, the tutor took the time to understand what was preventing Veronica from speaking English. Once he made her comfortable and came to understand her fears, he could create a safe environment for her to work in. Without this understanding, her teacher had jumped to an incorrect conclusion about her abilities.

Labels are not always negative, but all unjustified expectations are equally harmful. For example, to repeatedly call children "brilliant" or "the smartest in the class" leads them to believe that they must always meet these standards, not for themselves but for someone else. Such students learn to depend on that positive label and become more skilled at pleasing their parents or their teachers than at learning and pursuing their own natural curiosity and interest. Because their self-image is based on the opinions of others, positively labeled children often have the most fragile self-esteem and the most difficulty in learning to work for their own knowledge and pleasure.

Positive labels may thus be as unsubstantiated and damaging as negative labels. Although it is a good idea to bolster students' confidence and give them ample encouragement and positive reinforcement to aid their personal growth, tutors can do so without labeling. For, even when children do usually "live up" to their positive label, such labels can prevent educators from assisting the students in areas in which they are not as "gifted."

When you tutor, as you learn to work around the labels that the system places on students, you may find yourself coming to grips with some labels of your own. The following tutor was working with a group of "troubled" youths in an alternative high school. Although the tutor disagreed with the stated misconception that the students were "slow," in the beginning he did tend to agree that they were troublemakers and thus less interested in their education. Fortunately, he was open- minded enough to let them prove him wrong.

> Many students, I learned, were bused in from South Central, East L.A., and from all over the Valley. Although there were some students that would be considered "slow," many were actually quite intelligent. The problem was that their behavior was not tolerated elsewhere. Those who were bused in had to be on the bus by 5:30 A.M. This was a fact in itself that really impressed me. For students whom I had labeled unruly, the overriding fact is that they do care about education.

Putting people and things into categories is a natural process that we all engage in. We label and categorize to organize and simplify the world around us. But when working with students who function in a bureaucracy where labeling is an everyday necessity, it's important to try to go beyond labels and the convenient cubbyholes students are often sorted into. Every child has special talents and abilities, and it's up to the one-on-one tutors to discover and develop them.

What Can I Do as a Tutor?

Although the issues vary from case to case, you as a tutor may find your tutees' progress impeded by the adults around them. When this happens, tutors face a core dilemma: What can I do, and how can I help to alleviate my tutee's situation, without entering into a conflict situation with the significant adults?

There are not a lot of ways you can directly intervene in the interactions between your student and the other adults in their lives, but there are a few things you can do. You can *form relationships with their teachers and parents*, which will make these adults more receptive to your suggestions. You can *ignore the labels* that come attached to your students and form your own opinions based upon how they interact with you. And—the crux of the issue—you can accept them unconditionally, form strong relationships with them, and do your best to motivate them to learn and succeed in their ambitions. You can try to be the support they aren't getting elsewhere.

Forming Relationships with the Other Adults

The first and the most rudimentary action a tutor should take, beginning on the first day of tutoring, is to open an effective channel of communication with the "other adults." Parents, teachers, and administrators familiar with the tutor are more likely to give greater consideration to the tutor's concerns. Tutors make these connections most easily by being receptive and respectful to the other adults' presence and influence in the their tutee's life. It is considerate to fill them in on the progress of the tutoring relationship. Once tutors are perceived as the kind who take great pride and care in tutoring, they can expect their comments to be taken more seriously.

Most tutors who have constructed such channels of communication don't find themselves as helpless and frustrated about issues affecting their tutees. Many find that they can talk to the teachers or parents who are upsetting them. Talking doesn't always make a big dent, as the following tutor found when she did not necessarily change a labeling teacher's perspective, but she did get a chance to speak her mind.

> I was also able to talk to Mr. Morrison about Dustin this morning. He told me that Dustin has a big motivational problem. I told him that it was not evident to me on Tuesday. He read to me for over an hour and seemed to enjoy it. Mr. Morrison couldn't believe how much time he spent reading to me. He was pleased with my being in the class. Mr. Morrison said that now "Dustin feels like he has a buddy and that will be very good for him." He stated that Dustin can be a good kid when he wants to be.

The tutor in the next example had a much more successful response from the teacher she was working with. She found that the teacher appreciated her input as much as she appreciated being allowed to talk freely.

> For the past eight weeks, I have tried to keep Ms. Paul, the teacher, posted on Fernando's progress. Ms. Paul is a good teacher, but sometimes she tends to ignore the students that are behind in the course. I guess I can understand that she wants to keep the class interesting for the other students. But it finally got to me today, when Fernando raised his hand for the first time in the past eight weeks to answer the question, and Ms. Paul ignored him. I think she should have acknowledged the

significance of this occasion and let Fernando answer the question. So I decided to talk to her about what was bothering me so much.

As I went to fill her in on our daily progress, I told her about this situation. She paused for a moment, and then slightly hit herself over the head, and apologized. Apparently she is very overwhelmed with the class, and so used to my help with Fernando, that she unconsciously ignored him. She promised that she will encourage him to participate in the future sessions.

Had the tutor not developed smooth lines of communication with Ms. Paul, she might have hesitated to voice her concern or to run the risk of the teacher's misconstruing her comments as critical of the teacher's skill in the classroom.

Trying to Ignore Labels

Just because a student is handed over to a tutor with a label, positive or negative, doesn't mean that the tutor must act on it. Ideally, tutors treat all their students the same, starting out with a blank slate on each. Tutors give students a chance to prove themselves and encourage them when they want to challenge themselves. Sometimes the most important gift you as a tutor have to give is your unconditional support.

In the following example, the tutor was told that her student was a "slow" reader. The tutor chose to set the label aside as she began to work with the student and made her first project simply getting him to read with her so that she could see his abilities for herself. She found that his reluctance to read was based more on people's perception of him as slow than because he actually was.

At first, he was reluctant to read. I guessed that maybe it was because he didn't feel confident enough to read. I told him we could trade off paragraphs. Although constantly fidgeting and squirming, Manny began to read. He read very fluently and paused only on the most difficult words. The reason he didn't want to read was that he had already read that particular book and found it boring.

I was so impressed with his reading ability, mostly because I anticipated him being a slow reader. He didn't need my help in teaching him how to read. He was a fine reader and able to comprehend the material. So why was he stuck in a slow classroom?

This example shows how a label can lead teachers to have low expectations for their "slow" students. As a result, these students may be given material that doesn't push their limits. Once this tutor got past Manny's label of "slow" reader, the two moved on to work on spelling, writing poetry, and discussing newspaper articles. Soon Manny's father was frequenting the classroom and offering assistance to help Manny. The teachers were stunned.

The examples in this chapter have been aimed at illustrating some of the beneficial as well as harmful modes of interaction and influence other adults may have on your tutee's academic and social life. Not every tutor experiences them all, but it helps to anticipate the conflicts of interest that you and "other adults" may encounter as part of any tutoring situation.

As a tutor, at times you may feel helpless. You may feel that your student is caught up in a system that you are much too small to change or challenge. You may have no relationship with your student's parents. You may feel that your relationship with the teacher is too precarious to risk. Direct confrontation is by no means the only way to help tutees who struggle with the other adults involved in their lives. As an adult whom they may look to as a role model and mentor, you affect them too.

At the very least you will provide them with attention, encouragement, creative activities, and confidence—all things that the other adults may have taken away or withheld.

Recommended Reading

Scholars have done a massive amount of work on labeling. One of the classic works is *Being Mentally Ill* (1984) by Thomas J. Scheff. For an alternative view of labeling theory, see Howard Becker's *Outsiders: Studies of in the Sociology of Deviance* (1963). A dramatic and brilliant case study of the power of labels appears in David L. Rosenhan's "On Being Sane in Insane Places" (1973), which documents an experiment where "normal people" faked psychiatric symptoms to gain entrance to a mental hospital. After being admitted they couldn't get out, even when they acted normal and gave up their "symptoms." Rosenhan concludes that once a person is labeled "abnormal," others see all their other behaviors and qualities through that lens. Similarly, "K is Mentally Ill" by Dorothy Smith (1978) illustrates how easy it is to be labeled "ill" just by doing things differently than others, and how difficult it is to shake the label once it becomes a socially accepted truth.

Although "labeling theory" is often invoked in studies of the mentally ill, the theory applies equally to labels used to categorize students. "Slow learner," "low IQ," "poor background," "troublemaker," and "unmotivated" are examples of labels schools use that can haunt students for the duration of their academic careers. An excellent example of the changes in student and teacher behavior when negative labels are replaced with new, more positive labels ("gifted," "high IQ," "talented") is *Pygmalion in the Classroom* (1968) by Robert Rosenthal and Lenore Jacobson.

In "Student Social Class and Teacher Expectation: The Self-Fulfilling Prophecy in Ghetto Education" (1971), Ray Rist shows how kindergarten teachers categorize their students by the eighth meeting of class. Rist also reports how teachers contribute to the creation of the "slow learners" in their classroom by making these quick categorizations.

Students aren't the only ones the education system labels.

Parents and whole families are often labeled based on their race or ethnic group. This type of labeling can have a significant effect on the ways teachers interact with parents and the opportunities that parents have to help their children. In *Home Advantage: Social Class and Parental Intervention in Elementary Education* (1989), Annette Lareau challenges the common assumption that working-class parents value education less than do middle-class parents. Her in-depth ethnographic study shows that, although both groups value education, they have very different orientations toward it and different understandings about the appropriate extent of their involvement in their children's schooling. She demonstrates that some parents might need more instruction and guidance about their role in their children's education than others.

Finally, for an in-depth look at how the "other adults" in a student's life can affect school performance see *Unfulfilled Expectations: Home and School Influences on Literacy* (1991) by Catherine Snow, Wendy S. Barnes, Jean Chandler, Irene F. Goodman, and Lowry Hemphill, a study of varied scholastic achievement among low-income children. This book looks at students' interactions at home and at school as well as their families' relationships with the school; it offers important insights into how parents, siblings, teachers, and any adult can help improve children's reading. Among the suggestions: diverse and interesting educational and reading materials, consistent interaction with adults (especially helping with schoolwork and educational materials), and an emphasis on writing.

6
Good-byes: Ending the Tutoring Relationship

Forming a strong, successful tutoring relationship and overcoming the various obstacles in its way are among the most difficult tasks a tutor faces. Equally critical, and perhaps equally difficult, is ending that strong partnership. Saying good-bye, which signifies the end of the tutee's dependence on the tutor, is a milestone for tutor and tutee. Throughout the tutoring experience, tutors strive to help their tutees learn how to learn, adopt values that allow them to reach beyond what they were capable of in the beginning, and become self-motivated and self-sufficient. All these processes are transmitted through a partnership built upon trust and the dependence that trust allows. The ending stage of the relationship marks the tutee's final transition to independence.

Saying good-bye is a common feature of life and inherently emotional. Tutors therefore need to realize *the difficulties involved in saying good-bye and letting go* so they can develop an approach to it that is constructive and doesn't damage the student's memories of the relationship.

Being aware of how important and how difficult saying good-bye can be isn't enough. In fact, for many tutors this very understanding leads to *unfinished good-byes and harmful endings*. Often, owing to their own discomfort, tutors avoid saying good-bye, make empty promises, or create false expectations for their tutees. Any such action can make tutees doubt the whole tutoring experience. No matter how meaningful the tutoring relationship, ending it carelessly may leave the tutee hurt and regretful at having gotten involved in the first place, feelings that may affect their willingness to form relationships in the future and trivialize all they learned in the tutoring relationship; as the tutor, you might be cast as just another uncaring adult or unreliable role model.

The following scenario illustrates the importance of a good good-bye in the way Charmien, a nine-year-old African American student, greeted her new tutor: "She said to me, 'So, you're here for ten weeks like Megan, my old tutor, right? Are you taking the same class? Because I know you will be leaving after the class is over, aren't you?'"

It's apparent that because Charmien did not receive satisfactory closure from her former tutor, she now assumes that tutors are motivated by obligation, not caring. She has been left leery and suspicious. A strong good-bye must convey to the student that the relationship was very valuable—for both parties. It must also emphatically express that the tutor's leaving in no way reflects any negative quality of the tutee or the relationship. A good parting can leave a tutee with great memories of tutoring; a bad parting can leave a nine year old as jaded and cynical as Charmien.

Knowing *how to say good-bye*, then, becomes vital for any tutor. Saying good-bye can be a memorable experience, a ritual that leaves both tutee and tutor empowered and proud of what they achieved together. In the process, tutors help put things into perspective for their students and highlight the students' gains. Tutors also celebrate what the participants have meant to each other throughout the relationship. Overall, for effective good-byes, tutors take an honest, straightforward approach that respects the feelings of both tutee and tutor.

Endings make tutors and tutees sad. But, just as it is important to focus students on what they have gained from the tutoring relationship, it is beneficial for *tutors* to reflect on what they have learned as well. We know from the field notes of many tutors that tutoring is a *learning experience* that often proves to be a journey of self-discovery for tutors.

In approaching the issues of ending the tutoring relationship, we hope to guide tutors around harmful ways of saying good-bye and help them understand and deal with the difficulties of this process. There is no one best approach. As a tutor, knowing your tutee and understanding the tutoring relationship itself are your best guides. Nevertheless, one underlying principle holds for all instances: the best good-byes end the relationship honestly and cleanly.

Difficulties in Saying Good-bye

For many tutors, saying good-bye is the most difficult aspect of tutoring. Whether tutors work with individual students, small groups of tutees, or entire classes, a bond develops between students and tutors that prompts a sense of loss at the end of the tutoring period. Saying good-bye offers a host of challenges for tutors who wants to separate from their tutees in a manner that honors their relationship.

Feelings of guilt and shame sometimes overcome tutors, as they realize that their tutees didn't understand that they would not be there forever. Tutors have trouble breaking the dependence that their students have formed with them. As a tutor, for example, you may wonder how you can leave your tutees without your guidance. You may feel you are abandoning your students, and you may dread answering questions about why you are leaving.

The following tutor was working with two Latinas at an inner-city family center—Bertha, a seven year old, and Lila, a six year old—when she decided to stop tutoring because of other obligations. As she said good-bye, she felt guilty and worried that her tutees would feel abandoned. She questioned herself and wondered how her students would do without her help.

> As the end of the quarter draws nearer, so does the end of my tutoring experience, for now. I found it extremely difficult to tell the girls that I would not be coming back. I really want to return and I feel bad that I cannot, especially now that we are finally progressing. I keep thinking how they are going to have to start over again with a new tutor and how great it would be if I could just continue because they already know me, but I simply cannot. I truly will miss seeing them and I will wonder how they are doing and if their new tutor is doing okay with them. I hate good-byes.

To make saying good-bye even more difficult, tutees are often *reluctant to let their tutors go*. Some feel that they are being left behind or that their tutor is leaving because they misbehaved or did not learn fast enough. Others are just sad to see their friend and teacher leave. These are all issues that tutors should try to address in their good-byes.

No matter how carefully tutors plan, however , they may still be unprepared for their tutees' reactions to their saying good-bye, as was the tutor in the next example. She had been working in a classroom, and on the day she said good-bye, after the bell rang, the kids came flooding out of the classroom toward her. She hugged each of them, telling them to "Have a great summer" and to take care of themselves. She was unprepared for how unwilling they would be to let her out of their lives.

> We gradually made our way outside and I stood with eight or ten of them as they told me stories, grabbed my arm or hand, or tugged on my jacket. They told me how nice I looked, and how much they loved the treat bags I had brought them. After

awhile, five of them and I walked out toward my car. They kept me there for another forty-five minutes and surrounded the car so I couldn't leave. They sat on the hood or stood on the back bumper so I wouldn't drive away. I stayed until about 3:30 and then insisted that they get home. They groaned and asked for the millionth time why I couldn't stay.

As I pulled away, I honked my horn and they all stood next to the curb waving. About halfway down the street, I looked in my rearview mirror and they were all running behind my car. I couldn't believe how hard this was. I turned the corner and waved my arm out the window.

Other less dramatic reactions can be just as heart wrenching for a tutor who is already having trouble saying good-bye. The following tutor describes the reaction she received from her tutee: "When I told him I would not be coming back for tutoring, he actually looked and me and put his head down, saying, 'Man, you're the only tutor I really liked—you're the only one I really learned from.'"

Such reactions from tutees can be hard for tutors to deal with. These responses can't be soothed by kind words or comforting sentiments about the student getting a new tutor next year. They are individual and poignant reactions to one tutor's departure, and they can make a tutor feel personally responsible for the tutee's future progress.

Harmful Ways of Saying Good-bye

Seeing how difficult it can be to say good-bye to a tutee, it's easy to understand why good-byes don't always go perfectly. Tutors confronted with crying or disappointed students often feel helpless. In these moments there seem to be many ways to elude the hurtfulness of good-bye. In most cases these options avoid the short-term hurt but harm the tutee more in the long run.

To escape dealing with the emotional consequences of separation, some tutors completely avoid saying good-bye to their tutees; others avoid discussing the hard truth that they won't be returning. Still other tutors encounter situations in which they are prevented from saying good-bye, or from saying good-bye in the way that they planned. But whether a tutor intentionally avoids or unintentionally misses saying good-bye, the legacy of *leaving without saying good-bye* creates confusion and uncertainty for tutees. A tutor's sudden absence from the site makes it easy for tutees to assume apathy on the tutor's part. Not knowing the reason for the absence, they are likely to attribute it to their own shortcomings or failures.

Similarly, leaving tutees with *empty promises or false expectations* can soothe them for the moment but will leave them feeling disappointed and abandoned sometime in the future. As a tutor, It's better to let them be sad and upset while you are still there to explain what's going on and reassure them of the worth of the time that you've shared, than to have let them feel the loss of the relationship sometime down the road, when they can turn only to themselves for explanations.

Not Saying Good-bye

A common trap for tutors is the comforting thought that not saying good-bye will hurt their tutees less. They may think that it will be easier for the students if they "don't make a big deal out of it." Some tutors honestly believe that ending the relationship is a completely negative experience and. therefore, better taken lightly or avoided altogether. Others avoid the encounter because of their own anxiety. As one tutor explained: "Juanita looked indifferent when I told her that our sessions were going to come to an end next week. She seemed as if she didn't care. I figured that she doesn't want to make a big deal out of it. So, I decided not to talk about it any longer and we moved on with our activities."

In this example, even though the tutor notified the tutee ahead of time of his leaving, he avoided a discussion about the end of their relationship. Leaving the relationship with such an incomplete good-bye is not enough, however easy it appears, especially when the student seems apathetic. Children who look cool and undisturbed on the outside may still be overwhelmed by the stress of losing someone who cares about them.

Other tutors don't avoid saying good-bye but instead attempt to handle their good-byes casually. They don't want to make an issue of leaving and make their good-bye harder for the student, especially if the student is handling the situation privately. The following example poignantly illustrates that a tutee's silence may indicate that you as a tutor need to work especially hard to say good-bye and discuss your leaving and how you both feel about it. This white female had been tutoring Dustin, a Latino fifth grader who was considered a troublemaker, and had formed a close bond with him.

I usually leave the classroom at 10 A.M., but today I thought I would stay until recess at 10:15. About ten minutes after ten, Dustin said, "Samantha, look at the time!"

I said, "I know, but I don't have class today and since it's my last day here, I thought I would stay until recess."

The two girls in the group moaned and said, "Today's your last day? How sad."

Dustin didn't really respond at first, but after a few minutes passed he said, "Can't you just stay until lunch?"

I told him that I just couldn't because I had a paper to write and I had to finish it. I also said, "I am coming to your graduation though." Dustin got a big smile on his face and started cheering with his hands, saying, "Yeah!"

Mr. Morrison next dismissed the students out to recess. I asked Mr. Morrison if I could put some candy and a pencil on each of the students' desks. He told me that I could. The students came in from recess and were happy to see the candy and pencil on their desks. They started eating and sharpening their pencils right away.

Mr. Morrison then told the students that I would be leaving in a few minutes and if any of them wanted to talk to me, they could do that right now. Just as he said that, about twenty of the twenty-seven students in the class ran over to me at the back table. They all gave me a hug, thanked me, and asked if I was coming to their graduation. I could not help but notice that Dustin was sitting alone in the middle of classroom at his desk when all the students were gathered around me. I did not feel bad. Dustin did not have to come over and thank me or tell me he appreciates me and that I have influenced his life, I know I have, but I would have liked to give him a hug.

As I was getting ready to leave, Sean came up to me with a sad face, "Are you leaving right now?"

"In a few minutes," I said, "But we can read your book if you want."

"Okay," he said, as he ran to get his book.

As he was retrieving his book from his desk, Dustin walked over to me. He did not say anything or have his arms out-stretched for his hug. He walked over very slowly, had his hands in his pockets, and was looking down. I knew this was his way of saying good-bye. I reached out, gave him a hug, and told him that he made my time in Room 29 a lot of fun. He did not say anything, but did give me a small smile and went back to his desk. That was all I needed to make my time in Room 29 complete.

While Dustin's tutor doesn't "blame" Dustin for not being effusive with her, she also does not realize how hurt he is and how much the good-bye is affecting him. Fortunately, Dustin found the strength to make his own personal good-bye, but if he hadn't, his tutor might have walked out without hugging him at all. She had rationalized to herself that Dustin didn't have to make the effort for her; she did not realize that *she* had an obligation to make an effort toward *him*.

As a tutor saying good-bye, your feelings or comfort are less important than those of your tutees. Sometimes you have to go through an emotional good-bye that is difficult for you in order to explore their feelings and make sure that they understand what they meant to you and why you have to leave.

Many times tutors are unable to say good-bye owing to outside circumstances. The consequences of not ending the relationship cleanly can nonetheless be the same. Students who were absent on a tutor's last day may still feel abandoned when they return. This possibility underlines the importance of getting tutees' home-contact information—a tutor must make every effort to finalize the tutoring process, even if it becomes necessary to call the tutee. The tutor in the next case was able to convey a positive good-bye to her Latino fifth-grade student over the phone after she chose not to say good-bye because she had thought that she would be returning to the site.

(I call and he answers the phone.) "So, when does tutoring start?"

"Well . . . that's what I called about. I thought maybe Thursdays would work for me, but the scheduling didn't work out so I don't think I'll be able to tutor you this time. I'm so sorry."

"Really? Aw man, that sucks. Aw, what are we gonna do? Are you sure?"

"Yeah, I'm sure."

There was a long awkward silence. I wasn't sure if he was mad, sad, or just disappointed. I was all three. While faking a sniffle, he sarcastically said, "Oh, my, this is such a moment."

And then he started laughing. I was so relieved. "You little brat! You don't even care, do you?" I said sarcastically, laughing with him. "Did you even want me to come back?" By now we were both hysterical because we knew this wasn't the case. We knew that we'd really miss each other.

"Yeah, I'm gonna miss you. So, who's tutoring then?"

"I'm not sure, but I'll make sure you get somebody who'll give you a hard time and chase you around the school like I did, okay?"

After some small talk about school, soccer practice, summer, and work, we said good-bye.

No matter how it comes about (although preferably in person) tutor and tutee need time together to mark the final step in their relationship, and to celebrate the tutee's progress toward autonomy. It is this final step in the tutoring process that can either cement or unglue all the benefits of the tutoring relationship.

Making Empty Promises

When tutors do say good-bye, they often find themselves making empty promises to their students to alleviate the pain of parting. But empty promises can be as devastating as not saying good-bye at all. Promising to call, write, or visit a students, or giving them a phone number or address and permission to continue the relationship, can ease the situation in the moment but cause problems in the long run. In these situations, the tutee is left with the hope that the tutor will be back or that the relationship will continue. When neither happens, or happens but doesn't fulfill their expectations, tutees are left as confused about what their relationship meant as had there been no good-bye at all.

Empty promises come easy. The following tutor struggled to contain his emotions after informing his tutee that they would not be working together any longer and found an empty promise a convenient way to alleviate guilt and sadness.

> He gave me a long, soft look and then whispered, "I'm gonna miss you."
>
> I was fighting back the emotions and tried to keep my composure. "Yeah, me too." My voiced cracked, and I knew I had to say something to liven up the conversation, "But you know, you have my phone number and address, you can come visit or call anytime you want, and if we ever get our transportation together, then we'll be able to see each other."

Such promises, however sincere at the time, are generally impossible to keep. We all have busy lives full of obligations. Is a tutor really prepared for a tutee's call—"anytime"? No matter how great the temptation, tutors need to resist making these empty promises. They create false expectations for the students that can damage both their self-esteem and their future relationships.

Not only are false expectations disheartening, they may prevent tutees from progressing to the next step in the relationship: autonomy. Constantly hoping for a reunion or a phone call, tutees may refuse to put their old tutor-tutee relationship behind them. How deeply these expectations affect tutees is evident in the following tutor's experience: "I hate sharing Gilberto with his old tutor, Oton. Especially today, he was extremely sad and when I asked him what was wrong he said that Oton promised to call him yesterday but he never returned his call. I explained to Gilberto that maybe some accident might have occurred and that I am sure that he will call, but nothing seemed to matter. It was hard to connect with him as long as he was so preoccupied by his old tutor."

False expectations can be devastating. The best policy is to avoid situations that can lead to disappointment for the tutee.

How to Say Good-bye: The Clean-Break Principle

Following the clean-break principle is as simple as it sounds. As a tutor, end the relationship once and for all when you say good-bye. Be *kind* and *constructive* and *enthusiastic* about your students' accomplishments and their future. But avoid making promises to your tutees that you cannot keep—that you will visit or call, for example, or that you will tutor them again next year. It is better to be direct with your students than to leave them with lingering doubts or questions.

Even when there is a possibility that you might return to your tutoring, we advise you not to mention it. As one tutor explained, "I wasn't going to say I would see her next quarter because I didn't want to promise her anything I didn't know I could keep." If you come back, your tutees will be happily surprised; if you don't, you avoid setting them up to start the next school year with disappointment.

All tutors struggle with the pain of separation. In the following example, a tutor describes how, as hard as it was, he wanted to say good-bye the "right" way.

It was as if he could sense our time together was growing short. He reached over and grabbed my hand and, looking at me solemnly, asked, "Are you going to be around next year?"

I tried to recall how I was taught to say good-bye in lecture, and I began hesitantly, "Hiseo, I've had a great time working with you this quarter, but I'm afraid that I won't be able to come back next quarter."

He asked, "Why not?"

"I have too many classes to fit into my schedule and along with other activities I am doing, I cannot find a free block of time to come out here, like I did this quarter." I felt a little better knowing that I was being honest with him.

Being straightforward, sincere, and honest with a tutee is the best way to end the relationship. Even if tutors are preoccupied with hurting their student's feelings, by being genuine they help students to understand and grow through the separation process. Saying good-bye this completely can be painful for both tutor and tutee. But the beauty of the clean-break principle is that the tutor remains true to the values the relationship was built upon: respect and honesty.

At the beginning of the tutoring relationship, tutees become dependent on the unconditional acceptance of their tutors, and tutors become dependent on their tutees' feedback and reactions, which allow them to do the best job possible. Mutual trust and dependence make the relationship work. With good-bye, that dependence must end. But the ending should not leave the tutee feeling helpless and alone.

When saying good-bye, the tutor should aim to start the tutee on the road to autonomy, no easy task. Although 90 percent of tutoring time is allocated to building dependence, a tutor has only one or two sessions to work on this last stage. Among many ways to help bridge the gap between dependence and autonomy, some tutors find that bringing a small gift helps. *Gifts* can either symbolize an accomplishment that the tutor and tutee have achieved together, or the tutor's faith in what the student can accomplish in the future. *Talking about the tutoring experience*, capturing it positively, and making it clear to students that, as a tutor, you care about them deeply and think they are special and talented also helps fill the students with the confidence they need to step away from you.

Gifts

In ending the tutoring relationship, many tutors choose to give their tutees gifts that represent their relationship or small tokens to show their thankfulness for being able to take part in their tutees' lives. Such gifts need not be expensive or extravagant, but rather small and meaningful. In the next example, the tutor brought a gift that captured the relationship forever: "At the potluck, I brought my tutees little framed pictures of us with a note telling them each how special they were to me."

Other tutors bring presents more representative of the work that the two did together while tutoring, like the following tutor who gave her tutees artistic evidence of what they had accomplished: "I had gotten little notebooks of index cards and with colored pens had written all the words they had learned. I also wrote each one a personal note."

Another tutor brought her student M&M candy to symbolize the most significant feat of their relationship—conquering the letter *m*. By giving tutees a gift, tutors give them something with which to remember their tutoring experience. The gift serves to finalize the relationship, while keeping its memories and significance alive.

Gifts can also serve as visions of the future. Some UCLA tutors brought UCLA pencils or T-shirts to encourage their students' hopes of attending the university. The following tutor wanted her tutees to have presents to provide continuity over the winter break, so she brought them mechanical pencils like the one she used.

I decided to get them good-bye presents. I got each student the lead pencils, the ones they had asked for during my first tutoring session. Mando [a Latino nine year old] said, "I finally have a lead pencil, thank you so much! Can I kiss you? No one has ever treated me so nicely!"

I responded, "With this pencil, you will be able to solve every math problem. From now on math will never be a problem." As he smiled, I hugged him, and we quickly went to the other students to compare his new pencil. They were so proud of their new pencils, they continued thanking me and showing them off to other students. I was going to miss them so much.

The simple gift of the pencil made the children focus their attention on the positive aspect of the good-bye. They did not think of the time that they were going to spend away from their tutor but what they had accomplished and what they might accomplish in the future.

Talking about the Experience

An effective good-bye calls for a lot of talking—about the relationship and the separation process—focusing on the positive aspects of the tutoring and showing tutees that, no matter what, they will always carry a piece of their tutor. Tutors can show them that the tutoring relationship was a unique experience. The conversation might start with remembering the first day of tutoring, and go on to summarize and highlight the student's experiences and achievements. As a tutor, you can talk about the good times you had together, or bring up the special talents your tutee possesses. No matter what path you take, ending on a positive note works best. Show your tutees what they can take from the relationship to help them pursue their dreams and ambitions. You can leave them with an air of confidence, letting them know they are fully capable, on their own, of carrying on what you did together.

It's also important to talk about the end of the relationship before the last day. Sometime students have difficulty expressing themselves. Some need time to adjust to the fact that their tutor is leaving. Tutors can mention, a week ahead, that the last session is coming up. This gives tutees time to digest the information. It also gives them time to think about what they might want to say, or to bring their tutor a gift. It's common courtesy to give notice in the adult world, and it's a courtesy that we should extend to the children with whom we have formed these close and respectful relationships.

The following almost perfect good-bye, between a Latina university student and a male African American fourth grader, was marred by the student's suspension, just minutes before his tutor arrived. Although the tutor is somewhat cut off when her tutee has to leave early, and the mood is anything but joyous, this well-executed good-bye proves that even under the worst of circumstances, a tutee can leave a relationship with nothing but good memories and positive feelings.

Today was my last day going to tutoring. I had told Terrence before, so he knew. When I arrived, I told him, "I have something for you." I took out the candy and said, "Here is something sweet for a sweet guy."

Terrence reacted by smiling and opening his arms, walking toward me, and giving me a hug. As he hugged me, he told me, "Thank you." He looked at the candy, which was Hershey's Kisses, and said, "Ummmm! I'm going to put them in my backpack."

I told him, "Wait, here are some pencils I brought for you too." He took them, said, "Thanks," and went into the other room. When he returned he had a seashell. He gave it to me and said, "Here is a little something to remember me by." I reacted like he did because I did not expect it. I said, "Thanks, it's beautiful," and I gave him a hug.

The class had not returned from lunch. Sara and I were talking in the hallway. Terrence returned from putting away his candy and told us, "I have something to tell you."

I said, "Go ahead, what is it?"

He answered, "I got suspended today."

Sara and I were shocked; we asked him, "Why?" I was surprised because he was always very well behaved.

"I got into a fight. There is this boy named James in my class that is always teasing me because I'm darker than the other kids. I went up to him today during lunch and asked him, 'Why are you always calling me names?' James said, 'Get out of my face.'

I was about to move when he pushed me, so I pushed him back. I just got back from the office and they suspended both of us."

Sara and I looked at each other and did not know what to say. He was always so calm and polite. Sara asked him, "Did you tell anybody that he was teasing you?" Terrence said no.

I then asked him, "Did Mr. Grace know? Did your mom know?" He just shook his head from side to side. I told him the next time, he should tell someone if he is being teased by someone else. I said, "If you do not feel comfortable with a teacher then tell your mom. She should know." He responded with a whisper, "Okay."

I could tell that his suspension greatly affected him. He was always attentive during the tutoring, but today he kept looking at the floor and did not smile as usual. The candy had brought him some joy, but it had ended when he told me what happened. I tried to cheer him up by asking him, "What do you want to do today?"

He said, "I don't know." The fact is that he did not care.

I then said to him, "As you know, today is my last day. I want to ask you a few questions. Is that okay?" He said yes. I asked him, "What do you think is good about the tutoring? What could you improve?"

He answered, "Everything was good. I know how to divide." I asked him to elaborate and he said, "I know the steps without looking at the sheet." I felt good about his statement. It was this that confirmed to me that I had made an impact.

I told him, "I enjoyed working with you. You're a very good person. I especially like the poems you made about your race. You have a poetic instinct."

I was about to continue when an aide from the office came and said, "Terrence, your mom is waiting in the office."

Terrence told me he had to go. I told him, "Take care, thanks, and good-bye." He replied the same, smiled, and left.

Learning Experiences

Tutoring is a wonderful experience. Through their tutoring experiences, many tutors learn a lot about themselves, the environment in which they live, and the education system. Tutoring often opens their eyes to how much different communities need their help and inspires many to continue their work. One tutor wrote:

> Throughout this experience I have gained insight into myself and other's lives. This class and the tutoring has further encouraged me to work for the youth community and in education. Our students are thrown into a world they may not fully understand but experience every moment. All I know is that these students need love and encouragement, which they are not getting a lot of the time at school. Thus, the role of me, as a tutor, was to provide them with the encouragement and love they may have lacked in an academic environment.

This tutor has grown and learned from his experience and has realized that all it really takes to be a successful tutor is unconditional acceptance of tutees and the willingness to give them the care, attention, and understanding they need.

Another tutor had a change of heart after spending several weeks with his tutee. You may recall the following quote, used earlier in this manual, as the attitude *not* to have when entering a tutoring situation.

> I really wasn't happy with the school I was chosen to tutor at, and I was even less happy when I arrived at the school. I thought is this some kind of joke? I wondered, as I stood outside of the dilapidated school, am I even safe here? . . . I expected to be teaching highly motivated white students who were not just college bound but Harvard bound. I never even considered

teaching students that were minorities who might not even be interested in learning. . . . I had to ask myself, "What the hell am I doing here?"

As this tutor recaps his tutoring experience with a young Asian student named Hiseo, he shows that tutoring can touch the hearts of even the most reluctant converts: "When I initially began the tutoring project, I was skeptical about my chances of touching someone and affecting their life, but as I leave the program just a quarter later, I can honestly say that I have made a difference in Hiseo's life, and he has made even more of a difference in mine."

This tutor also wrote about how his tutoring experience opened his eyes to his long-held stereotypes of underprivileged children as lazy, stupid, and unmotivated. He ended his tutoring confident that he would one day teach in a community like the one he had tutored in, where students lack access to resources but are nonetheless hungry to learn.

Many tutors also discover part of themselves as they work with students. The following tutor rediscovered a childhood passion through working with an inspiring young student.

The decision to become a physician was not made until later, at age twenty-one, when I relearned from my six-year-old tutee, Collin, what it really means to do what I love—something that I had lost in the process of growing up! I started tutoring with the intention of giving back some of the opportunities society had given me. Never did I entertain the idea that I would benefit from this experience as well, by learning more about myself, my ambitions and desires.

I underestimated the emotional, moral, and intellectual power that the interaction with my tutee could bestow upon me. Until then, the idea of tutoring seemed a unidirectional act of giving. Little did I know that it was also about receiving and growing and that until I knew how to open up and learn from my tutees, I could not make a good tutor. . . .

Tutoring for me was like a journey, a journey of self-discovery that presented me with many unexpected challenges and learning experiences that let me grow, while allowing me to touch individuals that I would have never met or found something in common with had I not gotten involved.

Many tutors find so much personal satisfaction in tutoring that they cannot say enough good things about it, even if the experience is sometimes a difficult one. The following tutor has captured just a few of the moments that make tutoring so fulfilling.

If I were to have just a few "words of wisdom" unto you, it would be my suggestion that at one time or another in your life you experience the wonderful joys of teaching a child. Because, as Professor Rabow has said, it is you who will learn more and get the most out the experience. The child will learn but it will be you who will have the greatest sense of satisfaction and overwhelming pride. Especially at that point in time when she is struggling but you encourage her to keep trying, and she does and gets the answer to the subtraction or addition problem right (without using her fingers), she comes across that one word she continually cannot get and reads it naturally and without hesitation. You catch a glimmer of excitement and interest, and her face glows when she answers correctly, and for a brief moment there's a spark, and that is what makes it all worth it.

Through teaching another, this tutor clearly grew as well. She has discovered the profound truth that some of the greatest gifts in life come through giving oneself.

To realize the significance of the good-bye process and appreciate it's intricate nature, one should see the development of the tutoring relationship as a journey. As we move through life, encountering new and unfamiliar situations and obstacles, we follow a path of progress. We start out heavily dependent on another, one who knows the ropes, to guide us through. Ultimately, learning to navigate on our own, we arrive at autonomy.

Like other life paths, the tutoring relationship initially requires the tutee to rely heavily on the tutor. And, as in other successful journeys, the termination of this relationship marks the beginning of the tutee's independence. So good-byes are best regarded not as the end of a relationship but as progress—for the tutee.

Autonomy is one of the best things that any tutor could wish for a tutee, even though most of the relationship is dedicated to building a dependence based on trust. As you, the tutor, move through the relationship—teaching, supporting, motivating your student—you will be passing on the tools your tutees need to survive and succeed on their own. At the time of good-bye, they should be ready. So, tutors, cherish this chance and make your impact while you can, for missing the chance to say the right good-bye can undermine all the good of the relationship.

Children can handle the truth. The pain and difficulty of saying good-bye are inevitable. When you respect each other and allow yourselves to feel this pain, however, you both grow. It only hurts because you created a relationship, trusted, and impacted one another. It only hurts because you succeeded, together. Good-byes are neither unnatural nor to be avoided. Your good-bye is, instead, your last opportunity to share your thoughts, feelings, and encouragement with your tutees—and then let them go, to seek their own paths.

Recommended Reading

Robert Coles's *The Call of Service* (1993), a moving tribute to service work of all kinds, is an inspiring and thought-provoking book for anyone embarking on, or already entrenched in, volunteer work. Through the decades-long introspection of volunteers of all stripes, Coles offers many accounts of exciting and innovative tutors, teachers, and mentors, sure to help tutors improve their work.

In talking to volunteers ranging from civil rights workers in the segregated south to soup kitchen workers and tutors in Boston, Coles and the people he interviews dare to ask the big questions: Why am I doing this? What does it mean—to me and to them? What are my ideals, and what do they mean? Invoking a wide range of fiction and nonfiction and drawing on the personal stories of many volunteers, Coles captures the emotions, conflicts, and dilemmas of volunteer work. It is a book that anyone hearing the "call to service" should enjoy and learn from.

Twenty-Five Final Pointers for Tutors

- Treat your tutees as equals.
- Don't worry about mistakes—they provide the best opportunities for teaching and learning.
- Don't be critical of your tutees.
- Recognize your differences, a vital step to building a tutoring relationship.
- Recognize your commonalties, a vital step to building a tutoring relationship.
- Be supportive of tutees' efforts as well as of their accomplishments.
- Be hopeful.
- Make learning active, fun, visual, and hands-on.
- Keep your eye on the significance of your effort in your tutees' lives.
- Do not use bribes or gifts to motivate your tutee.
- Be willing to share your experiences when you think it's appropriate.
- Don't make empty promises.
- Don't forget how important you are—your tutee depends on you.
- Be on time.
- Use differences between you and your tutee to open up honest conversations.
- Forgive your errors and those of your tutee—they were unintentional.
- Be open-minded.
- Be empathetic toward your students and their experiences.

- Be observant and pay attention to what your tutees enjoy and how they learn.
- Incorporate tutee interests into your activities and assignments.
- Be creative.
- Set educated goals and strive for them.
- Ignore labels—they only show you part of a person.
- Be respectful.
- Remember that your students have much to teach you!

To the Reader:

We hope that you have found this manual useful and enjoy your own tutoring relationship. You may already have had unique and special experiences with tutoring and have developed specific ways of teaching and of developing relationships.

We would love to hear about any of the experiences that you believe might be useful to future tutors concerning your work with tutees, teachers, parents, and other adults. We invite you to share these experiences with us so that the readers of a sequel to this volume may benefit from them. You may e-mail us at jrabow@ soc.ucla.edu or tchin@ucla.edu.

For inspiration: One of the tutors, Brady Matoian, has prepared a video on the tutoring process. This twelve-minute video is available for $9.95 (including shipping and handling) from Professor J. Rabow, 10350 Santa Monica Blvd., Suite 310, Los Angeles, CA 90025 (California residents must add sales tax of 8.25%, or $10.77 total).

Thank you.

Bibliography

Ashton-Warner, Sylvia. 1963. *Teacher*. New York: Simon and Schuster.

Becker, Howard. 1963. *Outsiders: Studies of in the Sociology of Deviance*. New York: Free Press.

Becker, Howard, Blanche Geer, and Everett C. Hughes. 1968. *Making the Grade: The Academic Side of College*. New York: Wiley.

Cohn, Peter A., James A. Kulick, and Chen-Lin Kulick. 1982. "Educational Outcomes of Tutoring: A Meta-analysis of Findings." *American Educational Research Journal* 19, no. 2: 237–48.

Coles, Robert. 1993. *The Call of Service*. Boston: Houghton Mifflin.

Delpit, Lisa. 1995. *Other People's Children*. New York: The Press.

Dennison, George. 1969. *The Lives of Children*. New York: Random House.

Emerson, Robert M., Rachel I. Fretz, and Linda L. Shaw. 1995. *Writing Ethnographic Field Notes*. Chicago: University of Chicago Press.

Freire, Paulo. 1989. *Pedagogy of the Oppressed*. New York: Continuum.

Goodlad, John. 1984. *A Place Called School*. New York: McGraw-Hill.

Heath, Shirley Brice. 1982. "Questioning at Home and In School: A Comparative Study." In *Doing the Ethnography of Schooling*, edited by George Spindler. Prospect Heights, Ill.: Waveland.

———. 1983. *Ways with Words*. Cambridge, England: Cambridge University Press.

Herman, Rebecca, and Sam Stringfield. 1997. *Ten Promising Programs for Educating All Children: Evidence of Impact*. Arlington, Va.: Educational Resource Service.

Holt, John Caldwell.1982. *How Children Fail*. New York: Delta/Seymour Lawrence.

———. 1983. *How Children Learn*. New York: Delta/Seymour Lawrence.

Kohl, Herbert. 1967. *36 Children*. New York: Plume.

Kohn, Alfie. 1993. *Punished by Rewards: The Trouble with Gold Stars, Incentive Plans, A's, Praise, and Other Bribes*. Boston: Houghton Mifflin.

Kozol, Jonathan. 1968. *Death at an Early Age: The Destruction of Hearts and Minds of Negro Children in the Boston Public Schools*. New York: Bantam.

———. 1991. *Savage Inequalities: Children in American Schools*. New York: Crown.

Lareau, Annette. 1989. *Home Advantage: Social Class and Parental Intervention in Elementary Education*. London: Falmer.

Lewis, Catherine. 1995. *Educating Hearts and Minds: Reflections on Japanese Preschool and Elementary Education*. Cambridge, England: Cambridge University Press.

Miller, Alice. 1997. *The Drama of the Gifted Child: The Search for the True Self*. New York: Basic Books.

Natriello, Gary, Edward L. McDill, and Aaron M. Pallas. 1990. *Schooling Disadvantaged Children: Racing against Catastrophe*. New York: Teachers College Press, Columbia University.

Nieto, Sonia. 1996. *Affirming Diversity*. White Plains, N.Y.: Longman.

Rabow, Jerome, Hee-Jin Choi, and Darcy Purdy. 1998. "The GPA Perspective: Influences, Significance, and Sacrifices of Students." *Youth and Society* 29, no. 4 (June): 451–70.

Rist, Ray. 1971. "Student Social Class and Teacher Expectation: The Self-Fulfilling Prophecy in Ghetto Education." In *Challenging the Myths: The Schools, the Blacks, and the Poor*. Reprint series no. 5. Cambridge: Harvard Educational Review.

Robischon, Thomas G., Jerome Rabow, and Janet Schmidt. 1975. *Cracks in the Classroom Wall*. Pacific Palisades, Calif.: Goodyear.

Roemer, Joan. 1992. "Stars and Bribes Forever." *Parenting* 58 (October): 61.

Rose, Mike. 1995. *Possible Lives*. New York: Houghton Mifflion.

Rosenhan, David L. 1973. "On Being Sane in Insane Places." *Science* 179 (January): 250–58.

Rosenthal, Robert, and Lenore Jacobson. 1968. *Pygmalion in the Classroom: Teacher Expectation and Pupils' Intellectual Development*. New York: Holt, Rinehart and Winston.

Scheff, Thomas J. 1984. *Being Mentally Ill*. Rev. ed. Chicago: Aldine.

Smith, Dorothy. 1978. "K is Mentally Ill: The Anatomy of a Factual Account." *Sociology* 12 (January): 23–53.

Snow, Catherine. 1983. "Literacy and Language: Relationships during the Preschool Years." *Harvard Education Review* 53, no. 2 (May): 165–89.

Snow, Catherine E., Wendy S. Barnes, Jean Chandler, Irene F. Goodman, and Lowry Hemphill. 1991. *Unfulfilled Expectation: Home and School Influences on Literacy*. Cambridge: Harvard University Press.

Zemelman, Steven, Harvey Daniels, and Arthur Hyde. 1995. *Best Practices: New Standards for Teaching and Learning in America's Schools*. Portsmouth, N.H.: Heineman.